The Power of Pro Bono

The Power of Pro Bono:
40 Stories about Design for the Public Good by Architects and Their Clients

Edited by John Cary and Public Architecture
Foreword by Majora Carter

Metropolis Books

To Bob — 7. January 2011
With deep admiration & respect.
John [signature].

Contents

Democratizing Design

Foreword by Marjora Carter

One of my guiding principles is a phrase I first heard from a single mom in my neighborhood of the South Bronx. I was fortunate to meet her when I was running a nonprofit that worked to find environmental justice solutions to the area's economically and environmentally challenging conditions. She said, "You shouldn't have to move out of your neighborhood to live in a better one."

This notion has economic and environmental implications that span the globe. How we design and operate our built environment determines how people will move through it, to it, or out of it. When we let the design of our communities sink to the point where the only move people want to make is *away*, we create problems. Combining innovative thought with practical local knowledge dramatically increases the chances for something good to happen in those areas.

Too often, talented designers and the money to implement their creativity are not dispersed equally throughout our society—leaving portions of the population desperate to see something positive in their lives, while knowing that elsewhere (and not very far away), people are in more human-friendly surroundings. The good air, the green open spaces, the clean water, the healthy food, and the good design are all somewhere other than where these people are. This influences a person's self-image and many things that stem from it.

The global environmental problems we are beginning to face up to are a result of infrastructure design that treats poor people as less valuable than their wealthier counterparts. I imagine that if we had placed our transport, energy, waste, and agribusiness infrastructures within rich and poor communities equally, we would have had a clean, green economy decades ago. But we didn't.

This book shows how even seemingly small efforts can make people's day-to-day experiences healthier, more engaging, and more life affirming. It's unfortunate that these designers have to work pro bono. The product of great design has

lasting economic impacts that benefit some people directly and also benefit those who otherwise would be paying higher costs for social services but seeing lower educational outcomes and productivity. Well-informed, sensitive design can diminish the opportunity costs to a society that does not enable every person's creativity and passion to contribute to the greater good.

Recently I paid a visit to my former elementary school, P.S. 48 in the South Bronx, to dedicate the newly refurbished library, which is one of many libraries featured in this book, and which was designed on a pro bono basis through the Robin Hood L!brary Initiative. When I was growing up, the space was your standard public school no-frills library, but it worked for me, in part, because I was blessed with a very active imagination, a supportive family, and luck. Too many of my peers did not have those things going for them. We grew up when "the Bronx was burning," and many of the people around me died, went to prison, had babies at a very young age, or some combination of the three. How many would still be here if they had had this library and just that little extra safe space in which to dream? Where would they have focused their lives if their local environment had been filled with trees and green open spaces instead of diesel and power-plant exhaust and dangerous truck routes that lined their way to school? Although the Bronx is no longer burning, the hopes and dreams of many of our young people are.

Currently the U.S. holds about 5 percent of the world's population but produces 25 percent of its greenhouse gases. You might not know that 25 percent of the world's incarcerated population is held in the U.S., too. Studies by major universities have linked proximity to the sources of fossil-fuel emissions to learning disabilities in young children. Among poor children, the presence of these disabilities is a leading indicator of future jail time. A lack of green in people's lives also contributes to higher stress, lower self-esteem, and subpar school performance. These are all leading precursors of incarceration, domestic abuse, and increased high-school dropout and teen-pregnancy rates.

Our built environment *is* our environment, and we have some control over it as a society. The design projects in this book and the people behind them show how a select group of people chose to collaborate and improve our world. I hope that this pro bono phase is just the proving ground needed to demonstrate the true value of good design and its implementation. These projects are valuable for the people who plan and execute them and for those who experience the finished products in their daily lives.

We can achieve an America that is as good as its promise—but not by accident. I hope *The Power of Pro Bono* helps you dream bigger about where you are and talk about it with your friends, family, and others. That's how all great things start.

Preface by John Peterson

Because we should? Because it's good? Many would argue that all of us have a responsibility to "give back," and, moreover, that architects have a professional responsibility to provide services to those who can't otherwise afford them. This is a reasonable argument, and I generally agree with it. Yet this idea has done little to motivate me, and I don't believe it will do much to mobilize most designers.

Pro bono service *is* a good thing to do—although my definition of "good" may not be what you expect. While I don't want to undermine the importance of charitable intention, I do want to fuel the fire of charity by exploring other reasons why people might engage in this work.

"Greed Is Good"

I don't fully support Gordon Gekko's argument in the 1987 film *Wall Street*, but it can help expand the concept of good intentions. For instance, several times a week I run in the Golden Gate National Recreation Area, just across the Golden Gate Bridge from San Francisco. My friend Tom and I frequently end our run by walking a short section of beach, picking up debris along the way. Frankly, Tom began this tradition and he does most of the work. We don't get any recognition for our efforts, but one of our national parks is a little cleaner, and maybe there are fewer shore birds with bellies full of plastic.

Pretty selfless, right? Not really: I get a lot from this activity. I assuage the guilty feelings I have when I just watch Tom eagerly go at the task. I reinforce the sense of ownership I have for a place that has become like my backyard. And I simply feel a little better about myself. I don't imagine that many people would fault me for these selfish motivations, because the outcome is positive and there is a responsible balance between selfish and altruistic intentions.

All generous acts involve similarly self-serving motives. At the very least, they make us feel good. If we are going to get profit-oriented businesses, like architecture and design firms, to undertake the most pro bono service that they possibly can, then healthy, self-centered motivations are imperative.

Lesser Stepchild

To date, architecture firms and the profession at large haven't made very good use of pro bono service. There are, of course, exceptions, and this book is full of them. But pro bono projects remain the lesser-loved stepchildren of architectural practice. These are the projects that we typically fit in between our paying jobs, that don't make the portfolio, or that we hand off to the less experienced staff. We simply expect less from these projects. But we *are* being compensated for them, even if not in monetary terms. This is a core message of Public Architecture, the nonprofit organization that I founded in 2002, as we encourage architecture and design firms nationwide to formalize their commitment to the public good. We show firms that pro bono service is good for business, and we help the nonprofit and philanthropic sectors understand the valuable role that design can play in advancing their causes.

Over the years, just as we have faced reluctance from some leaders in the architecture profession about the need to formalize their commitment, we have found that nonprofit and philanthropic leaders are often so focused on the urgency of their day-to-day work that they can be slow to take advantage of opportunities that seem tangential to their primary task. For instance, they may find it difficult to invest in their own work environment when doing so would divert resources from causes like overcoming illiteracy or reducing domestic violence. Organizations shouldn't, of course, invest in facilities if doing so doesn't ultimately improve their bottom line: advancing their mission. But good design can do exactly that.

Not for Nothing

Pro bono service is an investment of architects' time and expertise. When we make an investment in a client, we bring something to the relationship that goes beyond the quality of service. This puts the architect and client in a relationship that is anchored by a shared goal or mission, as opposed to one that is structured by the exchange of fees for services. The architect comes to the table as more of an equal. As we are bringing an investment of in-kind service, we should, within reason, expect to have more influence over the selection and development of a pro bono project. Just as financial donors select and work with nonprofits to identify the best use of their money, architects can similarly guide the focus and use of their gift. This flies in the face of how architects typically approach pro bono projects.

Additionally, we often lower our design expectations under the misguided notion that the highest level of design is inappropriate for the populations that most nonprofits serve. Architects have had a troubled history serving these populations, and poorly conceived projects are often blamed on the arrogance of the architect. But our arrogance is not in elevating the design expectations; it is in our unwillingness to understand and embrace the desires of the people we serve. If the design does not respond to the particular needs of a community, it isn't good design.

Pro bono projects routinely generate deeper client/architect relationships than conventional fee-generating work. Often pro bono clients come to rely on their architects for a broader set of services, so that the architects find themselves in the role of a trusted advisor. One might think that this is about money: pro bono clients will ask for more services because they cost little or nothing. Cost likely has some influence, but the gift of the architects' time and talents conveys to their client that they are dedicated to the same goals. Pro bono or not, the trust of the client is the most significant component of realizing good architecture.

The pro bono relationship is not without its challenges. First, money is our society's primary tool to communicate the value and limits of service in most business relationships, and in its absence, a different but equally clear understanding of worth is needed. The simplest way to achieve this is to simulate the exchange of money, as John Cary describes in "How to Pro Bono," later in this book. Second, coming to terms with spending tens of thousands of dollars for design services helps provide the clarity of purpose and disciplined decision-making that a client must contribute to a project. Maintaining focus without this motivation is the most vexing problem to overcome; it requires continuous frank and direct communication between architect and client.

Designing for Need

Architecture has had an on-and-off relationship with the needs of those who inhabit the spaces that we create. Need seems too utilitarian for most architects; we like to think our goals are loftier—the meaningful expression of our culture, or the realization of an artistic vision. The architecture profession, too, prefers to celebrate the architect's role as artist over that of engineer or service provider. But need is not the enemy of provocative and poetic cultural meaning. It is the balance of all the complex issues within the built environment that makes architecture relevant. And while architecture may be the balance of art and science, the struggle is between art and service. How do we serve the needs of our clients and, at the same time, realize a vision that comments on and enlightens us as a culture? This is where the richness of architecture lies; this is where we find our true value. The projects in this book illustrate the breadth of impact that design can have.

Although virtually all architects believe that well-designed environments can have a profound impact on our lives, we have never felt compelled to prove it. Yet there is research that supports these beliefs. For instance, studies have shown that patients require shorter hospital stays when their rooms and furnishings are designed for social interaction, and they require less pain medication when their rooms have views of nature.[1] This sort of research is, however, very limited. I liken the attention we give the built environment to the case of nutrition. Although everyone believes that what we eat affects our health, it is only in the last several years that the mainstream medical community in this country has begun to recognize nutrition as a worthy area of significant research. Likewise, if we don't demonstrate the positive impacts of designers' efforts, we will never gain the trust and commitment of clients who serve millions of people in need.

Designer as Entrepreneur

There are effectively three groups that initiate projects in the built environment: real estate developers, businesses and organizations that construct their own facilities, and government agencies. Architects are rarely part of this process. Just as physicians help set the direction of health policy, architects should participate in identifying problems in the built environment. Some of the greatest value that designers can provide is to identify problems that others are unable to see.

Yet architects think of themselves not as problem identifiers but as problem solvers —culturally meaningful problem solvers, we hope, but problem solvers nonetheless. Someone hires us to tackle a desire, an obstacle, or a dream, and we go to work. Almost without exception, we wait for someone else to present us with a problem before we put pencil to paper or hand to mouse. Why must we wait? Do we not see worthy problems to solve on our way to work every day? What keeps us from throwing ourselves at them?

Once architecture firms decide to commit a portion of their time to pro bono service, they have eliminated the biggest obstacle, the requirement that paying clients approach them with projects. We are free to invest our talents where we

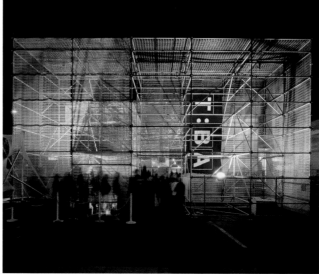

see fit. Pursuing our own project isn't easy, but it is deeply rewarding. It requires that we employ the entrepreneurial skills that are familiar to us but underutilized, like developing appropriate business models and convincing others with complementary expertise that a problem is worthy of their investment, too, because none of us can solve these kinds of issues alone.

The Undiscovered Country

Through my private practice, I have deeply enjoyed serving my clients over the years. Most of those clients have been part of the small group of people who could afford to pay my firm to design environments that expressed their desires and lifestyles. It was only when I tried to have an impact on the broader community that I felt the severe limits of the architecture profession's reach. A hundred years ago, architects embraced their role as civic champions; now we seem content to be discovered by magazines that only designers read, as our perceived value has increasingly been limited to three roles: risk management, entitlement facilitation, and market tastemaker. Through my work with Public Architecture, I have come to see pro bono service as a tool that enables us to immediately engage the wider population, which can't afford our services, and to begin to address the monumental need around us.

Although a few pro bono projects a year can't change the world, they can incubate models of service that are affordable to populations with limited means and attractive to the philanthropies that fund the social-service sector. There are millions of people who need the skills of architects, and, in much the same way that microfinance and other models of commerce have developed bottom-of-the-pyramid markets, there are vast opportunities for our profession. If we can abandon our entrenched professional limitations, stop waiting for the phone to ring, and embrace our ability to be entrepreneurial, then we can build a stronger profession and a better world.

[1] Roger S. Ulrich, "Effects of Healthcare Environmental Design on Medical Outcomes," in Alan Dilani, ed., *Design and Health—The Therapeutic Benefits of Design*, Proceedings of the 2nd Annual International Congress on Design and Health (Stockholm: Karolinska Institute, 2000), 54–55.

John Cary

Right now, in the Lower Ninth Ward of New Orleans, there's a new homeowner feeling grateful as he cleans his spacious kitchen, where he can cook a healthy meal, rather than warming up another microwave dinner in the FEMA trailer he occupied for years on end. There's a retiree in Brooklyn, sitting in a comfortable chair and surrounded by natural light, spending the day at her neighborhood's new branch library, reading and using the computers there to research her insurance needs. There's a pregnant mother in San Francisco, cradling her two-year-old in a warm, well-lit waiting room before her monthly checkup at the health clinic near the shelter where they currently live.

Spaces can enliven. They can excite the soul, fill us with a sense of wonder, and bring us comfort and reprieve. When planned with their ultimate users in mind, spaces become more than bricks and mortar and glass and steel; they become incubators for serving, working, learning, and loving. This is what architecture is all about—providing spaces that empower people to live their best lives.

Too often, we are subjected to, or settle for, private and public spaces that don't enliven and, instead, actually weigh us down. We grow so accustomed to the notion that doctors' offices and affordable housing developments can only be drab and unoriginal environments that we don't even dare to dream that they could reflect and bolster the spirits of those who frequent them.

In a single city, even just a few blocks away from each other, one fourth-grade classroom can be bathed in natural light, equipped with all the latest technologies that enhance learning, and filled with furniture and equipment that is easily reconfigured for the day's lessons, while another one has low ceilings, the glare and ever-present buzz of fluorescent lights, peeling paint, and graffiti-laced desks and chairs. There is a contradiction inherent in a society that tells our kids how important education is but sends them off to schools with abysmal classrooms, outdated libraries, and poor outdoor recreation areas.

These inequalities exist in urban, suburban, and rural communities alike. The reasons run the gamut from public policy to aesthetic taste to economic disparity, and blame cannot be relegated to any one party. The challenges for community centers, health clinics, libraries, parks, schools, and social service agencies, whose programs and resources are already stretched to capacity, are particularly troubling. These cash-strapped institutions provide critical services to scores of underserved people, who rely on them for everything from shelter and healthcare to childcare and job training to get them off the streets and back on their feet. With a majority of their patrons living at the poverty line or even without a place to call home, each of the buildings that houses one of these organizations becomes a refuge.

These spaces can go beyond the bare minimum of their intended purposes to become places that foster a sense of belonging and dignity. Rather than just adding some greenery to a block, a lively, thriving neighborhood garden can unify residents, pulling them out of their isolated houses and apartments and giving them a communal activity in a shared space in the public realm. Classrooms, where our children spend so much of their time, should and can contribute to the learning that happens within them. Instead of simply holding desks and blackboards, they can be designed to give kids comfort and inspiration that can build their confidence to ask questions and personally engage with the lessons being taught. In that way, they can help shape young adults and give them tools for continued personal and academic success. And for those students who need somewhere to go after the last bell rings for the day, colorful community centers can supply safe places to play as well as quiet spaces to study. Health clinics can offer emotional and physical comfort in addition to annual checkups, and public housing, beyond providing residents with a roof, can feel like home.

Few would doubt the value of places that achieve these goals, but the reality is that they are rare. That's where this book fills a void and raises the bar. The dozens of projects we have collected are tangible examples of how dignifying everyday spaces can enrich the lives of our kids, parents, neighbors, and ourselves. The stories of the featured projects are told from the perspectives of the determined designers who imagined them and the individuals who helped identify the intense need for these structures and have tirelessly seen them through to fruition. These projects serve as viable models, begging for imitation and adaption elsewhere in their own communities, cities, and states, as well as across our country.

This book is evidence that people at all income levels and nonprofits of all sizes have an appetite for and deserve quality spaces; that a great many architects have a strong commitment to the communities where they live and work; and that philanthropic institutions are willing to invest in realizing these places. The pro bono projects presented here show us the efforts of everyday architects to share their best skills and vision and who, in the process, often find a new dimension of personal and professional purpose. We also learn about the clients—the heads of community centers, children's camps, clinics, and food banks—who have commissioned and now work in these spaces, and whose spirit of service is as dynamic as the environments that surround them.

Creating Public Architecture

This book is inspired and informed by the activist design work of Public Architecture, a national nonprofit that architect John Peterson founded in 2002 and of which I served as executive director from 2003 to 2010. Public Architecture started with John's individual vision: that he, his firm, and the architecture profession at large had a role to play in making the world a better place. Public Architecture's work began modestly as a single public-interest design project and rapidly evolved into a bold advocacy agenda.

Around the time that Public Architecture was incorporated as a nonprofit organization, architect Tim Culvahouse, another one of the key people involved in its inaugural year, wrote: "Architecture doesn't just function; it expresses the human condition. It's about human dignity. It's about respect. It communicates identity and enables people to speak, to participate, to act. If you want to see what design has to do with identity, look at people's clothes, their cars. Architecture does the same things; it just lasts longer. Beauty dignifies, but architectural beauty isn't just in the look of things. It's the expression of who we are and what we value as a community."[1]

This statement aptly describes Public Architecture's mission. It also serves as a useful lens through which to view the more than forty pro bono projects in this book. These works represent the fruits of the pro bono design movement that Public Architecture has been leading since its inception, but the organization makes no claim to them. While Public Architecture undertakes actual design projects intended for construction, and a few of those projects are used as illustrations in this book, its real legacy is the intense interest and passion for pro bono service in the design community and nonprofit world. All of the projects presented here are potent evidence that architecture is a social act. Their successes demonstrate that we, as a society, can do better and that architects, as a community, should be at the forefront of helping communities bring about that change.

Cause, Not Cost

A wide array of projects, designed by architecture firms of all sizes from across the country, is presented in the pages that follow. They range from work by award-winning practices such as SHoP Architects in New York and Studio Gang Architects in Chicago, to young studios including Stephen Dalton Architects in Southern California and Hathorne Architects in Detroit, to some of the largest firms in the country, such as Gensler, HOK, and Perkins+Will. The clients include grassroots community organizations like the Homeless Prenatal Program of San Francisco, as well as national and international nonprofits, among them Goodwill, Habitat for Humanity, KIPP, and Planned Parenthood. Scores of private donors, community foundations and companies, and material and service donations made these projects possible. So have some of the most progressive funders in the country, ranging from Brad Pitt's Make It Right Foundation in New Orleans to the Robin Hood Foundation in New York.

Although much separates the many types of structures and spaces featured here, there's something that they all share: Each of them was designed at little or no cost to clients who could not otherwise afford them. They were designed pro bono. Pro bono is shorthand for the Latin phrase *pro bono publico*, which translates as "for the public good." While widely interpreted to mean "for free," the term goes well beyond the boundaries of free service and has a more complex nature than it is given credit for. The misconception that the term "pro bono" speaks of cost, not cause, is something that this book seeks to rectify. "For free" is everywhere in America; it is a part (and often a ploy) of our consumer culture. "For the public good" is something distinctly different. The projects selected for inclusion here demonstrate the impact and value of pro bono design and, specifically, its capacity to improve and change lives.

Pro bono service has been a hallmark of the medical world for decades, but it is most frequently associated with the legal profession, in part because attorneys are active in the promotion of pro bono service as a fundamental component of professional standing. Pro bono service is heralded in the bylaws of the legal profession: The American Bar Association (ABA) Model Rules of Professional Conduct encourages pro bono work, as do the state bars that ultimately license attorneys.[2] Pro bono service also makes its way into the daily operations of law firms and is an integral part of the culture. Many practices have full-time pro bono managers, pro bono partners, and even entire pro bono divisions. Few or no such equivalents

exist yet in the architecture profession. Perkins+Will is one exception, making some inroads through its Social Responsibility Initiative (SRI). It was the first large architecture firm to adopt a company-wide pro bono policy, and as part of that, it has appointed SRI officers in each of its eighteen U.S. offices and publishes regular reports on its pro bono work (see page 270 for more on the firm's efforts).

The legal profession's commitment to maintaining a pro bono culture is instilled in young lawyers early in their educations. Pro bono legal clinics are valued components of virtually every law school curriculum. While not mandated, this kind of supplemental service is what many top law firms look for when selecting new recruits. Similarly, law school graduates routinely evaluate a commitment to pro bono projects when choosing where to work.

Although architects have been doing pro bono work for decades, comparatively little can be found about it in their portfolios and client presentations. The Code of Ethics and Professional Conduct of the American Institute of Architects (AIA), a trade organization now over 150 years old, includes just one sentence encouraging pro bono service: "Members should render public interest professional services, including pro bono services, and encourage their employees to render such services."[3] (The words "pro bono" only entered the statement following a 2008 revision of the code.) There could hardly be a more striking contrast between this description of the responsibilities of the architecture community and the massive investment of time, financial capital, and human resources made "for the public good" by the ABA and the legal profession at large.

Are architects simply less altruistic? It's a harsh but necessary question when you compare the architecture profession with that of our peers in law. Why haven't we risen up and demanded that our work democratize access to well-designed housing, schools, and civic spaces in the same way that every individual in our country has access to legal counsel and protection under the law?

left
Perkins+Will
Business for Social Responsibility,
New York, New York. 2009

opposite
Chan Krieger NBBJ
Yawkey Distribution Center,
Boston, Massachusetts. 2009

The truth is that many individual architects and firms are seizing the idea of design "for the public good," but the practice isn't yet institutionalized or even very visible. Pro bono work also isn't recognized by the AIA or design publications to the extent that regular fee-generating work is celebrated. As a result, pro bono design has always been, and to a great extent remains, work that architecture firms do under the radar. The root cause may be timidity or humbleness on the part of firms, but it hurts the movement. Even an article in the *Boston Globe* lauding the Greater Boston Food Bank project, which is profiled in this book, made no mention of the fact that the building was completed thanks to hundreds of thousands of dollars' worth of services provided on a pro bono basis.[4] When queried, the architect said he deliberately downplayed his firm's pro bono contributions to avoid "muddying the waters."

Similarly, while doing research for this book, we found that very few firms included their pro bono projects on their websites, and when they did, they were rarely noted as pro bono. Why are architects afraid to take credit for, or even acknowledge, their valuable pro bono contributions? Even if unintentional, it is perplexing and greatly limits the awareness of pro bono design as a vital component and viable form of architectural practice. Externally, pro bono work has the potential to bridge a widely acknowledged gap between the architecture profession and the public by reaching a much greater percentage of the population than architecture touches today.

Pro bono service is increasingly being recognized as a critical component of a healthy business in other professions, even beyond law and medicine. One of the leading advocates for pro bono service nationally, cutting across many fields, is the Taproot Foundation, a nonprofit organization that mobilizes business, design, and marketing professionals to confer "service grants" to nonprofits in need. These are donations of social, as opposed to financial, capital. Since its founding in 2002, Taproot has engaged thousands of professionals to donate their time

and contribute their skills to strengthen hundreds of nonprofit organizations, ranging from well-known national outfits such as Rebuilding Together to local groups like Bay Area Community Resources. With offices in six major U.S. cities, Taproot is putting pro bono service on the map.

It's not just companies and nonprofits that are advocating for pro bono service, and it's also not a partisan issue owned by Democrats, despite President Barack Obama's resounding call to action. In November 2008, under then-President George W. Bush, the Corporation for National and Community Service—the government agency that oversees AmeriCorps, the Peace Corps, and other service programs—launched a major campaign called "A Billion + Change," which intends to push $1 billion in pro bono services into the nonprofit sector. The ongoing campaign elicits pledges from leading corporations such as Accenture, IBM, Intel, and Target. It was conceived following a groundbreaking study, "Capitalizing on Volunteers' Skills: Volunteering by Occupation in America," which mined three years of volunteering data from the U.S. Census and the Bureau of Labor Statistics.[5] The study concluded that although most people do not use their professional skills when they are volunteering, those who do are far more satisfied and more likely to continue those activities year to year. It turns out that pro bono work doesn't just benefit those who are served; it fortifies and inspires those who serve.

What Pro Bono Is and Is Not

For architects, pro bono work involves performing the professional and technical services for which they are trained and focusing them on clients in need. This distinguishes pro bono service from well-intentioned volunteer activities, ranging from participating in neighborhood cleanups to painting murals. Although it often is, pro bono service also should not be confused with other social activities popular among architects, like Canstruction, a competition in which architects

design and build elaborate sculptures out of cans of food, which are then donated to food banks and homeless shelters. The products of these activities demonstrate creativity and a commitment to helping others, but they don't constitute pro bono service.

The same can be said for the volunteer construction work done by architects, alongside people from many other professions and walks of life, for organizations such as Habitat for Humanity and Rebuilding Together. These remarkable nonprofits improve living conditions for thousands of people annually, but they rarely utilize the skills of architects, at least not at a significant scale. That is not to say that architects should not give their time to these important groups. In fact, in an attempt to spotlight the potential that can arise when architects become more involved in these types of organizations, four architect-designed Habitat for Humanity projects are included in this book. They are evidence of architects' ability to advance that group's design and sustainability agendas, even within the confines of its traditional material palette and largely volunteer labor force. As shelter is one of the most fundamental human needs, the possibilities for architecture firms partnering more actively with an entity like Habitat for Humanity cannot be understated.

Although it means much more than "for free," pro bono work does involve the rendering of professional services without expectation of a fee or with a significant reduction in fees for organizations and people who could not otherwise afford them. In the architecture profession, this work can take many forms but is generally any contribution of architects' professional knowledge, skills, judgment, and creativity that serves the public good. Some of the most common services are the same ones that architecture firms provide on a fee-generating basis. They include helping clients assess their facilities needs, producing printed materials and images to aid capital campaigns to raise money for building projects, integrating an organization's brand and logo into its physical space, making a structure

accessible to people with physical disabilities, as well as actually designing and constructing new spaces and buildings.

Public Architecture focuses primarily on 501(c)(3) nonprofit organizations—of which there are more than 1 million in the United States—as appropriate pro bono clients. Indeed, all of the projects we selected for inclusion here were undertaken by one or more nonprofit entities, such as social service agencies or schools. These organizations have been relieved of their tax burdens in recognition of the societal benefit they provide. According to the IRS, 501(c)(3) nonprofits may include organizations with missions that are charitable, environmental, health-related, religious, educational, or scientific, among others, although there are exceptions to this rule. Of course, not all nonprofits are equally in need of pro bono support; some have large endowments and extensive means. It is ultimately up to the design firm to decide how and where to donate its time.

A Movement in the Making

Community, humanitarian, and pro bono design are the three components of a growing movement aimed at making good design much more widely available. While their methods differ, all three share the motivation to democratize design. Naturally, each of these subsets of the public-interest design movement has its champions and challenges.

For more than four decades, small numbers of architects have organized themselves through Community Design Centers (CDCs). Among the first was the Architects Renewal Committee of Harlem (ARCH), cofounded by the late architect J. Max Bond, Jr. These centers, many of which were affiliated with architecture and design schools, practiced community design, often called "participatory design." They privileged the involvement of community members and users above all else, and many CDC leaders believed that approach distinguished their work from the work of mainstream architects and firms. This view created tension between CDCs and firms, and it devolved into a sort of class war between "socially progressive" and "design progressive" architects. The typical reduced-fee structure that CDCs employed also generated accusations from firms of unfair competition and undercutting of firms' fees.

Today we see new breeds of community design centers and programs that blend elements of each approach. Among the best known is the Rural Studio, cofounded in 1993 by two architects, the late Samuel "Sambo" Mockbee and the late D. K. Ruth. The studio is an Auburn University program that deploys students to design and construct homes and buildings in Hale County, Alabama, one of the poorest counties in the country. Building churches, homes, and other community facilities, the Rural Studio pioneered the idea that even the poorest in our country deserve and value good design. Before his death, Mockbee won a MacArthur Fellowship for his work with the studio, and in the years since its cofounders' passing, the program has continued to thrive under the leadership of architect Andrew Freear. The Rural Studio is widely admired and respected throughout the architecture community. Its work has expanded from single-family homes to civic buildings and spaces such as clinics, community centers, parks, an animal shelter, and a fire station. The studio illustrates the profound impact that architecture can have, even in just a single county.

Another prominent community design leader is Design Corps, a national organization founded in 1991 by architect Bryan Bell. Based in Raleigh, North Carolina, Design Corps undertakes projects for unorthodox client groups, such as migrant farm workers. Although many of the organization's projects are modest in scale, they are intended to be replicated in similar conditions elsewhere. Design Corps also innovatively places a small number of recent architecture program graduates to work in community organizations through the AmeriCorps federal service program. Additionally, each year, Design Corps convenes

hundreds of students and recent graduates interested in community design work at its Structures for Inclusion conference, with the goal of presenting public-interest design as a viable career path and mode of practice for architects.

Few CDCs, however, make it part of their practice to facilitate the involvement of mainstream architects at any significant scale, despite the number of architects who are willing and able to contribute their time. One of the only exceptions is the Community Design Collaborative in Philadelphia, which, since 1991, has carefully matched teams of architects and other design professionals with nonprofit organizations. The collaborative offers "predevelopment" architectural services at the beginning of a project's life, acting on the recognition that these nonprofits often have little funding available for this stage of the development process. Today the collaborative manages over 700 architects, landscape architects, planners, engineers, and cost estimators who devote their time and expertise to nonprofits in need of design assistance. In addition to numerous design initiatives, the collaborative takes on approximately thirty projects or service grants annually, matching professionals with nonprofits. All of this work is focused on the greater Philadelphia area, but the model is ripe for adoption in other cities.

The second subset of the public-interest design movement is humanitarian design, which involves disaster relief and design work in developing countries. Architecture for Humanity, an international nonprofit established in 1999 by architect Cameron Sinclair and journalist Kate Stohr, is one of the primary champions of humanitarian design. Since its inception, Architecture for Humanity has used design competitions to raise awareness about how architecture can respond to humanitarian crises. In its formative years, the nonprofit also pitched itself as a first-responder to natural disasters like the 2003 earthquake in Bam, Iran, and the 2004 Indian Ocean tsunami, and, on the domestic front, Hurricanes Katrina and Rita in 2005. More recently, the organization has created its Open Architecture Network, which is intended to "open source" design in the same way that the technology field has for software development. In the process, Architecture for Humanity has captured the attention of thousands of architects and students through highly decentralized, volunteer-run chapters around the world.

Architecture for Humanity is by no means alone in this pursuit. It is joined by many other groups, such as Architects Without Borders (whose name is a play on the well-known Doctors Without Borders), which works tirelessly to bring humanitarian design to developing countries.

The third component of the public-interest design movement is the subject of this book: pro bono design. It focuses on engaging and mobilizing architects and their resources and, in this sense, is the most scalable of the three branches. Rather than rely on the time and energy of volunteer chapter leaders, pro bono design is instead built on the same tried-and-true practices that architects employ to realize their fee-generating projects. It also doesn't position design "for the public good" outside of, or separate from, the rest of architectural excellence—instead integrating it holistically into architectural practice. It can also leverage material and service contributions from others in the building industry—contractors, engineers, manufacturers, and vendors—allowing it to expand beyond the boundaries of the architecture profession.

Community, humanitarian, and pro bono design—indeed, the public-interest design movement as a whole—evolved in response to the failure of the mainstream architecture profession to serve a much larger percentage of people than it has historically. Although the scale of engagement varies greatly, all three modes of practice benefit from the willingness of architects to put their professional skills to work for the public good—a public they themselves are a part of as coworkers, parents, and community members, blurring the line between the server and the served.

One Percent Pro Bono

In 2005, with the support of a grant from the National Endowment for the Arts, Public Architecture formally launched a national campaign called The 1% program, which challenges architecture and design firms to contribute a minimum of 1 percent of their working hours to pro bono projects. Since the program's inception in 2002, 1 percent was always meant as a symbolic rather than a literal number, and over the years, many firms have easily exceeded this intentionally low bar.

One percent of the standard 2,080-hour work year equals approximately twenty hours, a modest, but not trivial, amount of time. If all members of the architecture profession were to commit twenty hours per year, the aggregate contribution would approach 5,000,000 hours annually—the equivalent of a 2,500-person firm working full time for a year.

The 1% program aspires to significantly increase both the quantity and quality of pro bono work that is performed by architects and, ultimately, the broader design community, including contractors, engineers, interior designers, landscape architects, planners, and myriad other consultants. By making pro bono service a regular part of architectural practice, the program enhances the profession's engagement with the under-resourced communities where the projects are located. And by demonstrating the value of architectural services, The 1% program has increased popular awareness of the importance of good design in the built environment.

The program focuses on firms rather than individual architects, in recognition of the fact that the policies and practices of firms are crucial in making it possible and desirable for employees to undertake pro bono work. The same human resources, technical resources, and liability insurance coverage involved in regular fee-generating commissions are needed to execute pro bono projects. Philosophically speaking, the firm, at its best, is a microcommunity of professionals who can bring functional and innovative design to groups of people who are most in need of its benefits—and most often excluded from it.

In its early years, The 1% program grew gradually, thanks to commitments from a few dozen firms, including Oglesby Greene in Dallas and Pugh + Scarpa in Santa Monica. The Dallas-based firm of HKS was the first large, multioffice practice to sign on, followed by Perkins+Will, HOK, Gensler, and individual offices of other large firms such as SOM. Firms of this size effectively boost the hours and capacity of The 1% program and increase its reach through their networks of offices across the country.

In its first two years, The 1% program was simply an online venue through which firms could pledge their time and profile their pro bono philosophy and work. Following requests from both firms and nonprofit organizations, the program expanded its participant base in 2007, welcoming nonprofits to register their facility design needs. Through a matchmaking website—akin to an online dating service—The 1% program connects nonprofits in need of design assistance with firms willing to give of their time. The ultimate goal is to keep the number of available projects low, although several hundred can be found on the website at any time. Hundreds of completed projects and services are also catalogued on the site. These projects affirm the notion that there is a true need and demand for pro bono design, and they should serve as a call to action. As of this writing, in spring 2010, over 750 firms have pledged a minimum of 1 percent of their time through The 1% program of Public Architecture. This represents over 250,000 hours and an estimated $25 million in donated services—annually.

Forty Stories

Over the years, on its websites and in its presentations, Public Architecture highlighted a select few pro bono projects as exemplary. Some predated The 1% program, while others were products of it, but all were undertaken by firms on a pro bono basis. Among those singled out was Roxbury Estates, a ten-unit development in Seattle designed for Habitat for Humanity by Olson Kundig Architects, the 2009 recipient of the AIA Firm of the Year award. Others included multiple pro bono projects undertaken by the San Francisco firm of Fougeron Architecture for Planned Parenthood, as well as the fifty-six public school libraries redesigned through the Robin Hood L!brary Initiative in New York. These were, and remain, exceptional models of pro bono design, and all of them are featured in the following pages.

In preparation for this book, Public Architecture issued a call for projects in the hopes of identifying a few dozen more examples of pro bono work that had eluded us. We requested projects in which clear social relevance or benefit was embodied in the client's mission and the firm's commitment to the client's cause. We were also looking for a high level of excellence in architectural design and, of equal importance, a strong narrative, which could be conveyed through the perspectives of the designers and clients.

The response both inspired us and overwhelmed our e-mail in-boxes: Nearly 200 submissions poured in, on top of the hundreds already featured on The 1% program website. The submissions ranged from community centers and gardens to libraries and schools to houses and camps. Some firms included narratives about the philosophical underpinnings of their service pursuits, sometimes exposing common misperceptions and confusion about what actually constitutes pro bono work. Still, they all shared the goal of contributing to stronger communities.

The dozens of projects ultimately selected for publication best illustrate the triple threat of design excellence, compelling client stories, and positive impact on the lives of users. Some of them, like the work of the Make It Right Foundation, Planned Parenthood, and the Robin Hood L!brary Initiative, contain multiple projects, all of which not only fulfill our requirements but also demonstrate the exponential effect that can be created when clients and firms make sustained commitments to pro bono work.

While many conceptual and unbuilt pro bono projects had great merit, we chose to focus on built work in this book. We are largely invested in assessing real-world impact. But the importance of not-yet-built pro bono designs should not be overlooked; images of this work can be crucial as pro bono clients raise money to realize projects. For that reason, and because of their design quality, unbuilt schemes open each of the six project sections that follow.

Taken as a whole, the selected works represent six expansive categories, which are deliberately aligned with recognized divisions of the nonprofit sector and the expressed interests of most major foundations. Galleries, museums, and theaters are featured in the Arts section. Neighborhood parks and gardens and an urban farmer's market are among the projects in the Civic section. Community centers, cultural institutions, nonprofit offices, and social service agencies comprise the Community section. Child development centers, outdoor classrooms, and schools fall under the heading of Education. Clinics, redesigned hospital rooms, and a recreational facility are in the Health section, and finally, a collection of single- and multifamily homes makes up the Housing section.

All told, these projects represent tens of millions of dollars in donated services and materials. Even more significant, they also represent collaborations forged, communities strengthened, and lives improved. The projects demonstrate that

worthy causes deserve and thrive in supportive, inspiring spaces. Reflecting on the processes that brought all of these designs to fruition, it is clear that nonprofits can be invaluable clients and partners for those in the for-profit world, and that, in partnership, the design community and the "do good" community can become indispensible to one another. Together they can catalyze systemic change, empowering people to live their best lives.

1 www.publicarchitecture.org/about/What_We_Dont_Believe.htm.
2 www.abanet.org/cpr/mrpc/mrpc_toc.html.
3 www.aia.org/about/ethicsandbylaws/index.htm#P3_417.
4 Robert Campbell, "At New Food Bank, Good Work Inside and Out," *Boston Globe*, Oct. 4, 2009.
5 www.volunteeringinamerica.gov/assets/resources/VolunteeringbyOccupation.pdf.

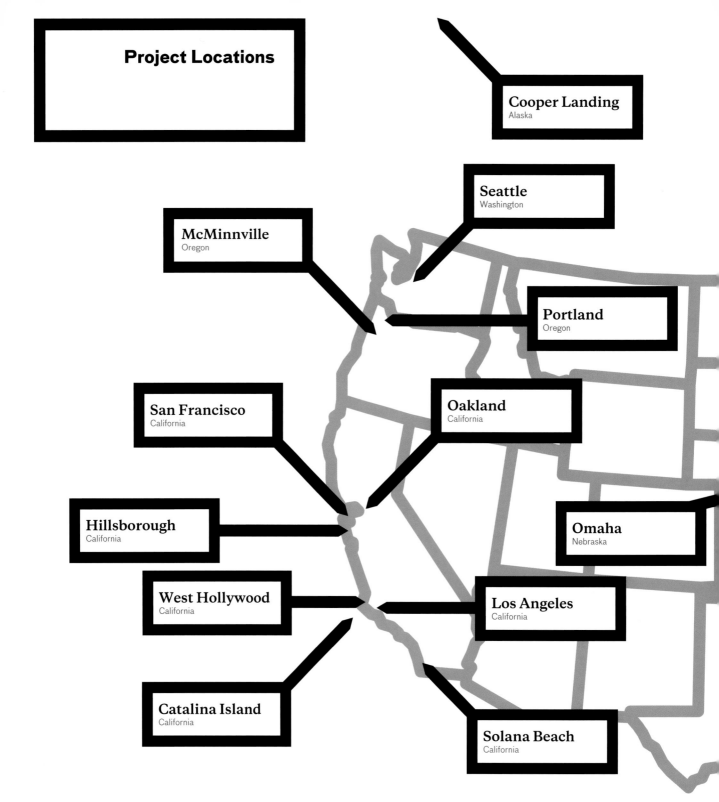

Project Locations

Cooper Landing
Alaska

Seattle
Washington

McMinnville
Oregon

Portland
Oregon

San Francisco
California

Oakland
California

Hillsborough
California

Omaha
Nebraska

West Hollywood
California

Los Angeles
California

Catalina Island
California

Solana Beach
California

Minneapolis
Minnesota

Middletown
Connecticut

Amherst
Massachusetts

Boston
Massachusetts

Royal Oak
Michigan

New Haven
Connecticut

Detroit
Michigan

New York
New York

Chicago
Illinois

Washington
District of Columbia

Fayetteville
Arkansas

Atlanta
Georgia

Pass Christian
Mississippi

New Orleans
Louisiana

Houston
Texas

Arts

Fusebox

Fusebox Gallery
Location Washington, D.C. **Date** 2001 **Client** Fusebox Gallery **Client liaison** Sarah Finlay **Design firm** CORE **Design team** Dave Conrath, Peter Hapstak, Brian Miller, Thomas Quijano, Dale Stewart **Area** 1,500 sq. ft. **Cost** $102,000 **Estimated value of pro bono design services** $15,000 **Website** www.coredc.com

Sarah Finlay
Founder, Fusebox Gallery,
Washington, D.C.

CLIENT

Washington, D.C., as a city, never had much light industry, so there are not many big spaces for arts organizations to occupy. There is also a real rift between the gallery and museum worlds. The city has wonderful museums, but for galleries and collectors, it has always been second tier because of its proximity to New York. I had worked in other galleries in the city and met a lot of talented artists in the community—some amazing younger artists, as well as midcareer artists with teaching positions at the Corcoran College of Art + Design and the Virginia Commonwealth University—but they were selling to a limited group of local collectors.

I realized that a major reason many people in the city, especially younger collectors, didn't participate in the art market was because they were intimidated. They would ask, "How do I know that I'm making the right decision?" My cofounder, Patrick Murcia, and I wanted to open a space where patrons felt welcome and artists and curators felt wanted.

When we started looking for a home for the gallery, we did not have many local models to follow. There were many tiny, jewel-box-like spaces in the Georgetown and Dupont Circle neighborhoods of D.C., but not much more. Patrick had worked in community development and had written about the U Street Corridor, an interesting part of Washington with deep history. It had been part of Black Broadway, one of the most famous intellectual and cultural African American communities in the country in the early twentieth century. We decided that would be the perfect place for our gallery. ▸

Peter Hapstak
Principal, CORE,
Washington, D.C.

ARCHITECT

The art scene in Washington, D.C., has always been a little frenetic. It is a transient city, and because it turns over every four years, the environment for art never really jells consistently. Fusebox cofounders Sarah Finlay and Patrick Murcia came into this environment, and they brought a wealth of knowledge about art. Sarah had educated herself on what was happening in Miami at Art Basel and what was going on in Europe and other places around the world, and she wanted the gallery to reflect that. The people they wanted to showcase were doing much more abstract work than most of what you see in this city. Some of the stuff was really out there, so we got a crash course in the local art scene.

The project was very urban; it wasn't meticulous. There were flaws. From our standpoint, it's not a perfect world, so we don't try to build perfect architecture. The building itself was a retail space on 14th Street. It had sound bones; we were kind of lucky that we had this box that was inherently intact. We focused a lot on light. The walls were evenly illuminated to see the work in the most minimal ▸

way. For the floor, we used concrete board, which is frequently used as siding on homes in areas prone to inclement weather. We screwed 4-by-8-foot sheets to the floor, so the whole space got an industrial feel from that.

What made the gallery really unique was the idea we developed to create a pivoting wall. It became the signature element of the space. The wall rotated 360 degrees on a car axle and large ball bearings that we had set into the floor. It was really amazing that you could push the wall with your finger, and it would fly. If you turned it one way, it created a large opening on one side of the room; turned the opposite way, it created an equal opening on the other side. ▷

If you placed it parallel to the wall, it opened up the whole space. The gallery could change its shape and accommodate larger projects or gatherings of people.

Not only did CORE design the gallery, but we built it as well. We have taken on that role in the past with other projects, but we don't do it on a regular basis. We had a young associate, Dave Conrath, who was trained as a contractor before he went to architecture school. He did much of the building, and he was relentless. He really fell in love with it. We saved Fusebox an enormous amount of money, and I think Dave made it possible for everybody to come together and get it executed. ▸

Sarah and Patrick were trying to create a progressive institution in a conservative city, and it was really challenging. As their reputation grew, the gallery's events were more and more packed. So many people would be standing around that the fire marshal would have to break up the crowds. Fusebox was a catalyst for many changes in the neighborhood.

We took possession of a space in July 2001 and started demolition the next month with the help of Peter Hapstack and CORE. The property we found had been fallow for six years; it was in terrible condition, and there was junk everywhere. We pulled out the ceiling to reveal the existing wooden beams, because we wanted to show some of the history of the building. It was so beautiful, and those beams ended up being amazingly useful.

We also needed a place to store the art that was not on display. I had worked in galleries where the art was wrapped in bubble wrap and then shoved onto shelves. It was awkward, inaccessible, and the art was often damaged. With Peter, we worked out an idea for racks that came out on tracks in the floor. They slid out silently, and the work then could be mounted on them, opened, and unwrapped. It sounds minor, but it was important to what we were trying to create. The little galleries in Georgetown and other parts of the city always had cramped back offices where the deals were done, and we wanted everything in our space to be very open.

We opened the gallery two weeks after 9/11, which was a crazy but wonderful experience. We were in the neighborhood working for hours and hours, day after day. The owner of the liquor store, which had been there for years, was so excited and optimistic about what was happening that he wanted to make his own improvements. He had this horrible, old metal sign that was hanging from one screw on the front of the store, but the day before our gallery's opening, he was out there with a contractor and wanted our input on his new sign. It was really sweet. We had entrenched ourselves, and the arts, in the community.

Green Street

Green Street Arts Center
Location Middletown, Connecticut **Date** 2005 **Client** North End Action Team **Client liaison**
Izzi Greenberg **Design firm** Centerbrook Architects and Planners **Design team** Russell Learned,
Mark Simon **Area** 15,000 sq. ft. **Cost** $1.5 million **Estimated value of pro bono design services**
$130,000 **Websites** www.greenstreetartscenter.org, www.centerbrook.com

Mark Simon
Principal, Centerbrook
Architects and Planners,
Centerbrook, Connecticut

ARCHITECT

Middletown is a large town, almost a small city, and it has one district, the North End, that is home to a relatively disadvantaged community. Wesleyan University has a very vibrant arts department, and organizing arts programs was something the school could offer that part of the town. Wesleyan is only a few blocks away from Main Street and the North End, so the university was keen to make an improvement that would benefit the town and its own campus.

NEAT has worked hard to increase the amount of affordable housing in that district, and the team's original vision was to have arts facilities that were flexible and could be used by many different people. The idea was to teach classes for kids, and then in the evenings, the space could be used for adult education. We knew building the center would be a tough project in terms of budget, but solving difficult problems is rewarding to us. ▶

Izzi Greenberg
Executive Director, North End Action Team,
Middletown, Connecticut

CLIENT

The North End Action Team (NEAT) is comprised of people who live in and are committed to the North End neighborhood of Middletown, home to Wesleyan University. In many ways, our neighborhood has an unfair reputation; it's considered the wrong side of the tracks. It is also one of the most ethnically diverse neighborhoods in the region, so it's been a good place for Wesleyan University students to get involved in the community. NEAT, in partnership with Wesleyan and the city, decided that the neighborhood needed a community center.

There was no place that was safe and engaging for families and youth in the community to spend time. Our main goal for the center was to ensure that kids feel connected to it and that it could be used by a variety of different people for different purposes. We wanted the neighborhood to have ownership over the building. We also wanted to make sure that the building itself fit into the neighborhood and not stick out like a sore thumb.

We quickly identified the site: a structure that had been home to an old school. It was rickety and had undergone a horrible internal renovation in the 1970s. Centerbrook's architects were conscientious about trying to keep its historic bones while creating a modern space. They also worked to ensure that it remained an open design. Instead of having a walled-off space at the entrance where there would normally be a reception area, there is a smooth transition into the building.

Our focus was on creating a safe and engaging place for the community, so during the design process we constantly asked questions like: "Is it welcoming? Is it open? Will people want to spend time there?" We interfaced with people in the neighborhood to make sure that they were happy and felt involved, and that effort paid off. Since opening, the Green Street Arts Center has been very successful. It has a specific focus ▶

The city donated a Victorian building that had been a school but had not been occupied in years. Our firm is interested in the reuse of old buildings—our own office is in an old factory from around 1900. The building dictated much of what could happen and where, but throughout the process, we kept in mind that spaces would be used in different ways at different times.

The older part of the school had high ceilings, so we used part of it to make a large dance studio. To make it flexible for other uses, we painted it dark, almost like a black box theater. We even designed a curtain system that could go across the windows and darken the room entirely. The high rafters in that space allowed us to install theatrical lighting.

We took a number of old classrooms that faced north, including one that had a skylight, and turned them into art studios with nice, even light. There are small music rooms that we made soundproof for private lessons, and we created a funky recording studio where the kids can make music. Those spaces don't need much daylight, so they are on the lower floors.

NEAT also saw the arts center as an opportunity to provide after-school help, such as mentoring and tutoring, for local children. What we call "the café" does double duty; it is a lobby, where people wait for classes to start, but it's also a study hall. We were very security minded, so whoever ▸

on the arts, but it has served lots of functions within the neighborhood. We have used it for community meetings, an after-school program, and adult finance classes. NEAT and Green Street together ran a sort of youth invention group called the DaVinci Club, in which the kids learned construction and built a club house. A lot of the kids in that program helped paint the light fixtures at the center. Almost every parent in the community wants his or her child in that kind of program, and it has become a great entrance point for the rest of the family to use the center. They spend time there and spread word about it to their friends.

During the design and building process, the NEAT team worked to ensure that Wesleyan University was responsive to the needs and desires of the neighborhood. The university had a reputation of not coming off the hill to be a part of Middletown. This project started to change the city's impression of the university. NEAT already had a mentoring program that paired Wesleyan students with children in the community, and now they meet at the art center. Professors, who might have been hesitant to be in this neighborhood because of its reputation, come here and meet the families, which changes their opinions about the North End. That goes a long way toward breaking down mostly unfair stereotypes that historically have plagued our community.

is at the entry desk can see who is coming and going at all times.

The project as a whole was on a real shoestring budget. The irony is that low-budget projects sometimes require more work than those with big budgets because you are trying to make something out of little or nothing. We were concerned about how we would finish it, but we were also determined to be clever and solve problems.

In a number of places, we left pieces of the old building exposed. For example, we found a pair of blackboards—the old-fashioned kind with lines for kids to practice handwriting—so we built around them. We made the windows in the doors round and playful, and they're different sizes depending on the room. We had fun making the place feel special within the tight budget. But, in the end, it was our interaction with the people who use the space that was the most rewarding element. All sorts of people who might not normally be involved got involved and made something together.

Halcyon

Halcyon Playhouse
Location Fayetteville, Arkansas **Date** 2009 **Client** Court Appointed Special Advocates of Northwest Arkansas **Client liaison** Crystal Vickmark **Design firm** Maurice Jennings Architect **Design team** Maurice Jennings, Walter Jennings, Lori Yazwinski **Area** 121 sq. ft. **Cost** $10,000 **Estimated value of pro bono design services** $8,000 **Websites** www.nwacasa.org, www.mauricejennings.com

Crystal Vickmark
Executive Director, Court Appointed Special Advocates
of Northwest Arkansas,
Springdale, Arkansas

CLIENT

Court Appointed Special Advocates (CASA) of Northwest Arkansas is one of 900 such programs in the United States that recruits, trains, and supports community volunteers who advocate for children in foster care. The children have most often been abused and neglected and are no longer safe in their homes. We believe that every child should have a happy and safe childhood.

For about seven years, we have been running a fund-raiser called Playhouse Palooza. In it, local builders construct playhouses that we auction off, and the proceeds help fund our organization. The program has raised over $400,000 to support our cause. The playhouses are a metaphor for the sense of safety we want to give children, and the sales of the structures help provide for the kids.

When the playhouses are completed, they are set up for two weeks in the local mall. They're configured as if they are a small neighborhood, with potted plants, trees, and mailboxes in front of the houses. Each house also has advertising in front of it and spec sheets with the same kind of information you get when you buy a home: the amenities of the house, who designed it, who built it, and the estimated cost. On the Saturdays of those weeks, we hold an open house where visitors can walk through the playhouses. They are asked to vote on their favorite houses and make comments about those they liked. We end the event with a live auction of the houses. ▸

Walter Jennings
Maurice Jennings
Architect,
Fayetteville, Arkansas

ARCHITECT

The purpose of the playhouse project is to raise money and awareness for CASA. To do that, the organization has several builders, architects, and people in the community design and build playhouses that are then displayed in the local mall. To make money, the houses are auctioned off later in the month.

Before building our playhouse, we had heard about CASA's work in the community, but it was Neal Hefner, a contractor we had worked with previously, who got us involved in this project. Neal approached us about working together; he thought this would be a way to do something different than a house or chapel, which are the typical structures we design and build. We all thought it sounded fun.

From the start, we knew we could make something that inspired more imagination from the children —something that could simultaneously be a stage, a hideout, a house, or just a sculpture. There were a lot of constraints from CASA in terms of space. ▸

The team there needed to be able to move the piece into the mall and show it off, so we had to stay within a 9-foot cube. We prioritized having different degrees of openness within the structure. Kids can crawl up on the top and have a privileged view out, or they can go underneath to peek through the lattice. If they want to hide, they can crawl in the back, or that area can act as the backstage if they are putting together a performance or playing make-believe.

To approach the design, we got together with Neal and sketched out on a napkin what we thought we could do in our cube. We had a palette of materials from previous projects to work with, and Neal had some leftover pieces from a cedar shake roof. There were several extra sheets of plywood and pieces of cypress wood, and we knew a metal fabricator who could donate some of his time. His material was all water-jet cut, and it shows up well when the sun is setting.

I think the interesting thing when working with volunteer design and labor is that you don't have as much control as you would on a paying job. When you pay someone, you can tell him or her to build it as it is drawn. However, with this kind of project, we say, "We have a little opening in the next week, and we could knock this one out pretty quickly." In the end, we had something that we were really happy with. ▷

We have requirements for the playhouses in terms of dimensions and safety. Builders need to use Plexiglas instead of real glass. We also ask them to keep in mind that their clients are children, with short fingers and legs. Doors should not be heavy, handles should not be too high, steps should not be too tall. Builders are encouraged to be very creative within our guidelines. Many choose to collaborate with architects, design firms, and even interior decorators to make the playhouses special. We came in contact with architect Walter Jennings through one of our builders, Neal Hefner.

Compared to our other projects, the structure Walter and his team developed is unique. We mostly see pavilions, barns, or replicas of trees, and everything here is very different. This is the first time that we have had anything of this caliber and style. The bold color is great and the openness is soothing. This playhouse could fit anywhere, in nature or a residential neighborhood. Several adults commented on how this would be great to use for both children and adults. You could sit out there and have a cocktail in the evening or coffee in the morning. It appealed to all generations. Walter put his heart, soul, and imagination into this pro bono project. It is not your cookie-cutter playhouse.

This was the largest pro bono project we had done. Our other work was small: for example, a basic sign for the school district and playground equipment for Greenland Public Schools, here in Arkansas. This project gave us the opportunity to show a different side of design than we normally do. Sometimes you get known for doing what you do well—in our case, chapels and houses. That is good, but it is nice to show people that you can do something else.

p:ear

Suzanne Blair
Jessamyn Griffin
Christina Tello
Designers,
SERA Architects,
Portland, Oregon

p:ear Gallery
Location Portland, Oregon **Date** 2009 **Client** p:ear **Client liaison** Beth Burns **Design firm** SERA Architects **Design team** Suzanne Blair, Jessamyn Griffin, Christina Tello **Area** 5,258 sq. ft. **Cost** $523,000 **Estimated value of pro bono design services** $60,000 **Websites** www.pearmentor.org, www.serapdx.com

ARCHITECT

We were sold the second we met the p:ear staff. They're such a dynamic group, and what they've built in the past seven years is pretty incredible. Their dedication to their mission really resonated with us.

Initially, our firm sought out pro bono work through personal connections, which yielded a handful of projects that we considered taking on for our commitment to The 1% program. By chance, one of our coworkers was at a fund-raiser and chatted with a p:ear staff member. She mentioned the group was looking for design services, and it just kind of fell into place. From that point on, it was obvious that p:ear was the right choice for us. We had other great project opportunities, but the organization was in our community, literally down the block from our office.

We employed the same integrated-design process that SERA Architects uses for almost every project. To get started, we organized a design charrette with the p:ear staff and board of directors. We are used to charrettes and building consensus, so we re-created that environment for p:ear, being careful to make sure the process wasn't intimidating but instead was more hands-on, and, honestly, more fun. Getting everyone together to talk really helped move us forward. ▸

Beth Burns
Executive Director, p:ear,
Portland, Oregon

CLIENT

We started p:ear (which stands for program: education, art, and recreation) about ten and a half years ago as a small nonprofit serving homeless youth. We had been running an alternative school for homeless youth through the Portland public schools, but the Salvation Army decided to close our program, so we started p:ear.

For our first independent facility, we wanted street-level access, many windows, and enough space to have lots of us in one room—to create a community, eat together, and share our lives together. What we ended up with was the ground floor of an abandoned building that had flooded two years before we moved in. Whenever it rained—and it rains a lot in Portland—water came through seven floors and dripped into our space. There were two toilets and one sink with only cold water. The kitchen consisted of a microwave and a toaster, but we somehow managed to serve 12,000 meals a year. Then, after six years, we found out we were losing the space because the building was being turned into a boutique hotel, and it became severely rat infested as they started construction.

Our space had to represent the aesthetic and values we bring to the kids. We are asking young people to re-evaluate themselves and how they feel about their community. A really beautiful, light-filled space is the place to start that process. I swear, almost immediately after learning we needed to find a new home, we got a phone call about a building that was up for sale. When we walked in, my cofounder and I didn't say a word to one another. When we walked out, we said, "That's it."

The building was divided into two big squares. We had this completely blank slate. One square had a mezzanine, which instantly we thought could be the office. The back space, the second square, had a big garage door. It fulfilled two functions: It let us participate with the program below sound-wise, but it also gave us some separation and privacy. The building would provide a huge amount of space for our art gallery and art-supply storage. We found the space in November 2008, and put it in escrow for six months to see if we could raise the money to buy it.

During that time period, at a fund-raiser dinner party, I met an employee from SERA Architects. At a subsequent meeting, we told SERA that we had this beautiful space but no money, so they took us on pro bono. ▸

Since we are all fairly junior staff, we decided we needed to pick a mentor within the firm, someone who would guide us through the process, cross our t's, and dot our i's, but not take over. Tim Richards, a project architect at SERA, was kind of like our visiting professor; we'd do most of the work and then every couple of weeks show him where we were, and he would give us comments. His goal was to help us learn how to manage the process and take control of it.

The hardest and most important part was getting the contractor, because while it's great to be architects and draw things, we needed to get this built. We had originally worked with a different firm on pricing at ▸

a schematic level. However, that firm donates to a lot of other public service agencies around town, and it was kind of tapped out that year in terms of pro bono work. We were really disappointed at first. Then we had one of our principals at SERA make a call to Fortis, and it turned out the president of that firm was interested in the project. That was a critical link and moment. In the case of all the other consultants, we pretty much just asked them, and they said yes.

In the design, there are two main program areas. The front room houses the kitchen and p:ear's main activities. The majority of the kids hang out in that space. There's also a library, a quiet study room, a computer room, restrooms, and a mezzanine with offices. The other section of the existing building is a former garage, which we converted into a gallery. It's more of a public space, and it's where p:ear hosts its "First Thursday," a monthly event open to the public that shows the kids' art along with that of local artists.

Giant folding doors open up to the street. When you walk by on those nights and the space is all lit up, it feels really welcoming. At the first opening, an artist came in and painted a big mural all over the walls. It was something p:ear couldn't really do in the other space. The flexibility of the space now is, by far, much better than what the organization had. The open kitchen is at the heart of the building. ▸

The project incorporated donated items and salvaged building materials, so it ended up having a really cool, funky personality. That feel emerged because we didn't have a lot of money, and things couldn't be ultramodern or sleek. We utilized salvaged doors, windows, and lumber, and specified local, regional, recycled and low-emitting materials. While p:ear decided not to register the project with LEED, we did pursue tax credits and grants for some of the improvements made to the building. We had to roll with what we had.

We all cared so much about the success of the project. We really believe in p:ear's mission, the people we worked with, and what they are trying to do. We appreciated their dedication to us, too. They weren't trying to get the cheapest project possible; they were trying to solve their problems and create this space with us.

One of the first things they did, which was definitely the most crucial part of the entire process, was sit down with us and run through exercises to help us clarify what we wanted. Out of this exchange, we came up with the idea to try to market the space and rent it out. I think we've rented it out twenty times in the last six months for $1,000 per event, which is really good money for us.

When the architects at SERA designed the space, we still had no contractor, so they brought on Fortis Construction to do the project. Fortis was amazing; the employees have so much heart and donated most of their costs. We were given the phone number for each subcontractor, and before Fortis accepted bids, we called each of them to ask if the firms would donate part of their services, so that cut costs tremendously. The folks who did the casework donated tens of thousands of dollars' worth of time and materials.

Since we moved in, there has not been one time when we said, "We wish we had done this; we wish we had done that." The prep work SERA did with us—particularly the firm's constant questions about our vision for the space—was amazing and created a product that is 100 times more functional than our last space. The kids are spending a lot more time here. Our old space would get crammed really quickly, and kids would bolt. The kitchen creates a very homey, nurturing, caring environment. A lot of the kids we work with have been living in extreme poverty their whole lives. This space acts as a central hub and home base for hundreds of kids throughout the year. They rely on us.

Prospect.1

Prospect.1 Welcome Center
Location New Orleans, Louisiana **Date** 2008 **Client** U.S. Biennial **Client liaison** Dan Cameron
Design firm Eskew+Dumez+Ripple **Design team** Steve Dumez, Nicole Marshall, Thaddeus Zarse
Area 300 sq. ft. **Estimated value of pro bono design services** $22,000 **Cost** $30,000 **Websites**
www.prospectneworleans.org, www.studioedr.com

Dan Cameron
Director, U.S. Biennial,
New York, New York

CLIENT

The idea for the biennial in New Orleans came to me about five months after Hurricane Katrina roared through the Gulf Coast. In terms of bricks and mortar, I felt we, as artists, weren't the people to rebuild New Orleans; that is for other people. Instead I wanted to create a signature event and develop something that the city could rally around culturally. Through a series of attractions that focused on contemporary art, I believed there was a way to draw to New Orleans the tourism that comes with successful biennial events. We looked at models, like the Venice Biennale and the São Paulo Biennale, and worked to create something comparable.

Eskew+Dumez+Ripple (EDR) first became involved casually in the summer of 2007, when a mutual friend invited Allen Eskew and me to dinner. We got to talking about what would become Prospect.1, the first art biennial in New Orleans. It would be organized under the auspices of U.S. Biennial, Inc., and Allen offered to help in any way, such as securing permits or doing actual design work. We met again soon after, and during the course of a two-hour meeting, EDR divided our approximately twenty requests into four categories. The process had the potential to be messy and complicated, but the firm sorted it out from the beginning and came up with a plan.

We found the historic Hefler Warehouse on Magazine Street, and the owner signed a six-month lease with us for $1. The space was very bare bones; it was a big, open, empty warehouse, with no interior walls. It was also dark, cold, dusty, dirty, and a bit damp. Allen evaluated the space with us and then started having meetings with different architects on his staff. We had a lot of space, but more than that, we had a very open-ended set of needs.

The architects got a sense of our requirements, but we really wanted to treat them as artists in the exhibition and give them creative control. We were not just a client; we were partners in the project. As a curator, it is my role is to bring out artists' best—to get an artist excited about and invested in a situation. The proposal that I presented to Allen and ▶

Steve Dumez
Design Director,
Eskew + Dumez + Ripple,
New Orleans, Louisiana

ARCHITECT

All three of us who are principals at EDR are members of the boards of different organizations in the community. As part of that service, we tend to do pro bono work—not just consulting work but actual design services, design reviews, and constructability reviews. Allen Eskew, a principal here, is a board member and past president of the Contemporary Arts Center in New Orleans, and he came in contact with Dan Cameron.

Dan approached Allen about us helping on the Prospect.1 biennial project, initially just ▶

managing permit questions for the sites. There were eighty-one separate art installations scattered around New Orleans. Some of those projects were in found spaces, unutilized or underutilized buildings that were reopened just to hold an installation. In a lot of cases, these areas were still somewhat devastated by Hurricane Katrina.

Some money emerged from the Downtown Development District to help Prospect.1 finance a welcome center. Located in the Warehouse Arts District—part of the Downtown Development District—the center would be a jumping-off point for visitors to find information about the biennial and the arts community in New Orleans. The district offered $10,000 to help put together the project.

By the time Dan found the spaces and organized the events, the opening was probably about eight weeks away. That is when Dan engaged us to help with the welcome center. Allen was very concerned about our ability to pull off the construction, but I thought we had to do it, since it was clearly an important art event. Our firm has designed a number of galleries and museum facilities both locally and regionally. We are invested in the arts community, and I knew we had a lot to offer.

It was difficult to assess what could be done because the U.S. Biennial didn't have a real budget— just this $10,000, which had to pay for not only the center itself but also ▸

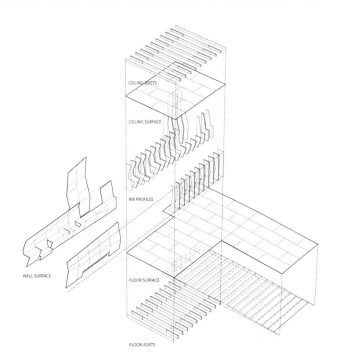

CEILING JOISTS

CEILING SURFACE

RIB PROFILES

WALL SURFACE

FLOOR SURFACE

FLOOR JOISTS

some upgrades to the warehouse site. There wasn't really any sense of the true cost.

In the end, the welcome center was designed and built within a seven-week period at a low budget. Very early on, we got involved with a contractor who was interested in doing small work. Together we came up with a strategy to use just one relatively inexpensive material: plywood. We developed a way to construct it and came up with the concept of making it look like fins on the outside and then shaping the wood to act as structural ribbing to support the interior wall. There was a nice dialogue about plywood and the relationship of a wooden box within a timber warehouse building.

We were quite lucky to have a client who was not challenged by a strong concept. Since he's a curator, Dan has a sophisticated eye. As soon as we came up with an approach that was somewhat unconventional, he was ready to embrace it. Convincing a client to go out on a limb sometimes is an issue in and of itself. This wasn't an issue with Dan.

The real struggle was with budget and security. The warehouse's main entry was a roll-up overhead door. We needed a new front door that telegraphed to the outside that something special was happening within and that was also operational in inclement weather. We came up with an iron gate faced with a translucent polycarbonate, on which we printed large graphics ▸

themed to the event. At night, there was a constant glow coming through the doors, which made people wonder what was going on inside. Even just slightly ajar, the new doors allowed glimpses in and gave off a sort of mysterious quality. Having to find a solution for something as prosaic as replacing a garage door gave us an opportunity to add something significant to the space.

The public relations benefit to our firm from this project has been significant. We submitted it to some interior-design awards programs, and it clinched the first two, from *Contract* and *Interior Design* magazines. It is terrific to see that kind of benefit from a donation of services. You cannot buy that kind of press. Pro bono work is a chance to get involved in the community in a way that is important. On that level, the benefits are both personal and professional.

his partner Steve Dumez was really along those lines. I said, "If you could make a fantasy out of this project, what would that consist of?" I knew they were creative and had a clear sense of New Orleans and the architecture.

EDR's design for the welcome center for Prospect.1 was very simple but gorgeous. As you entered the warehouse building from the front door, you faced the actual welcome center structure, which was about 40 feet away. It was perfectly framed inside the space; you could see all of it. People were viscerally involved in the approach. Crossing those 40 feet, getting closer and closer, was really a lot of fun. The contrast between the warehouse and the structure was compelling. The only thing that I would have done differently would be to push the scale out a bit. The piece could have been a little larger, a little more looming and monolithic, though it had a fantastic aerodynamic sharpness to it. With other work on display, there was art, but, really, it was a place where we wanted people to have a look around, sit down, and take a load off.

From this project, I have learned that the interaction of art and architecture doesn't need to adhere to the typical boundaries. The overlap between the two fields used to make me nervous. I worried that art would end up losing its autonomy and its role when combined with architecture, but this particular collaboration has helped me leave that feeling at the door. I'm now much more interested in these kinds of partnerships. In fact, I would love to see an architecture biennial in New Orleans on the off-years of the art biennial, as is the case in Venice. New Orleans is a really exciting place to be in terms of architecture and design. When there is so much happening, it doesn't take much to kick off some of these ideas. Prospect.1 was a free event—there was no admission charge—nonetheless, it generated $25 million for New Orleans.

Soft Cube

Soft Cube Gallery
Location Omaha, Nebraska **Date** 2008 **Client** Bemis Center for Contemporary Arts **Client liaison**
Hesse McGraw **Design firm** Min | Day **Design team** Jeff Davis, Jeffrey Day, Drew Seyl, Maura Trumble,
Eric Zuerlein **Area** 2,466 sq. ft. **Cost** $2,000 **Estimated value of pro bono design services** $16,500
Websites www.bemiscenter.org, www.minday.com

Jeffrey Day
Principal, Min | Day,
Omaha, Nebraska

ARCHITECT

I have been involved with the Bemis Center since 2001. The opportunity actually came about accidentally; I met some people who worked there, and they were interested in expanding the programs in the center's existing building. Previously they only made use of the basement and two of the five other floors in the building. I started talking with them about collaborating with Min | Day and engaging architecture students to help keep costs down. Out of this relationship with Bemis, we developed the FACT program—which stands for Fabrication and Construction Team— through the University of Nebraska-Lincoln, where I teach. The program works to engage architecture students in our pro bono work. At the time, though, this was our firm's first experience with a pro bono project.

We determined that what the center needed first and foremost was a master plan for the entire complex. We shifted gears ▸

Hesse McGraw
Curator, Bemis Center for Contemporary Arts,
Omaha, Nebraska

CLIENT

The Bemis Center is a contemporary, multidisciplinary arts center that was founded in 1981 as an artist-in-residence program. We invite about twenty-four artists annually to live and work here for three months at a time. When I began working at the Bemis Center, I was quite fortunate to discover that Jeff Day was heavily involved with the organization. Jeff was doing high-caliber work nationally and previously had worked on architecture and design projects for the center. He and I began talking about other design possibilities that could be integrated into existing programs here.

At that time, one of the three galleries in the center's 10,000-square-foot exhibition space was unscheduled for an entire summer, and we had the idea to do a twelve-week event series instead of a gallery exhibition. We called it "Endless Summer," and it consisted of concerts, performances, lectures, and special screenings. The problem was that the area was a gallery space, essentially a drywall box. Jeff and I were worried about the acoustics for the programs and discussed what could be done to address the sound problems.

That conversation expanded to address what kind of architectural intervention could happen within our gallery to make it more suitable for events and gatherings. Min | Day jumped on the idea of altering this space, now known as the Soft Cube Gallery. Initially, when we began the conversation, we were talking about a temporary installation, something that would only remain through the completion of "Endless Summer." When that ended, however, we realized that turning the gallery into an event space better took advantage of the square footage, and that Min | Day's installation really supported that use. ▸

from a design/build project to a planning project. Our work with Bemis evolved over time into a host of different projects, some of which have come and gone because of changes in the organization's overall mission and its understanding of the space. However, even these unbuilt projects help us understand how the staff uses the space. In one case, we designed a store for the center to sell catalogues and books. After a trial run, the employees decided they weren't prepared to actually run a store. So our design work, at times, leads to decisions *not* to do things, which is pretty interesting.

The idea for the Soft Cube Gallery began over a lunch meeting with Hesse McGraw, the center's curator. He told me he was planning a series of events in one of the galleries and wanted to do an architectural intervention to support a greater variety of activities. To add fuel to the fire, the project had to be finished within two months of that meeting. We started thinking about how we could fix certain aspects of the space so that it could become more conducive to public activities. Everything also had to be flexible so it could be reconfigured depending on the performance. Out of this came the most prominent feature of the gallery—what we call the "soft wall."

The primary function of the wall is to serve as an acoustic baffle. It doesn't have any parallel surfaces, which is a way to bounce the sound around. The structure is made ▶

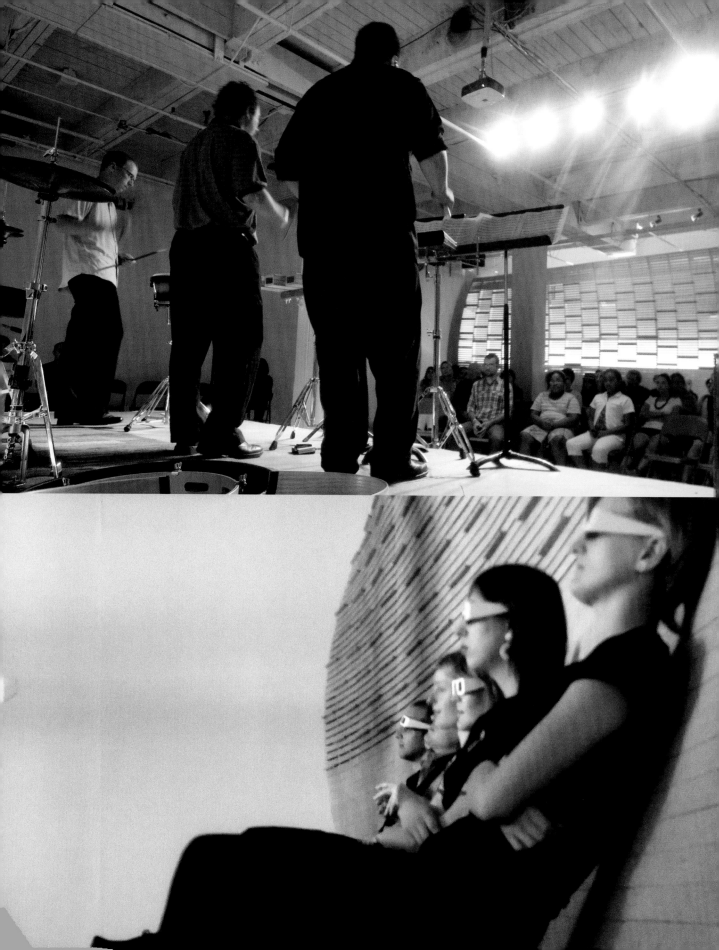

It took less than two months to complete the renovations. Min | Day had a number of summer interns from the architecture program at the University of Nebraska–Lincoln, and their work helped the process move quickly. The students were paid through a grant, so Jeff was able to work with them on the design development, and then they actually built the Soft Cube Gallery elements on the site. They produced a combined unit that we call the "soft wall." It's composed of a sound baffle with a lighting element and a bench. They also created a stage and a curtain that separates the backstage area.

The stage is built modularly, so it can be reconfigured depending on where events are taking place in the building. It has been quite useful for us. The soft wall has become a permanent fixture. Depending on what is happening in the space, its character can be changed by something as simple as turning the lights on and off. The installation is neutral enough that it doesn't overshadow the event. That concept was based on my first conversation with Jeff about ideas for the center, and it really brought about a shift in the program as a whole, not just the space.

What we have with Min | Day is not a traditional client-architect relationship; it's much more along the lines of a curatorial conversation. Over the last year, our staff at the center has started to address some basic circulation issues for the first floor of the building. We've been consulting with Jeff throughout that process, and at a certain point, it gave rise to a conversation about how we could change the entire entrance to the building. We are thinking about how you put people on their toes as they enter.

The interesting thing about our collaborations with Min | Day is that they can happen on multiple levels. It can be a floor plan improvement that costs a few hundred dollars; the Soft Cube, which cost a few thousand dollars; or something much larger, like long-term capital improvements to the building. That sense of scalability is key. If we're trying to support exceptional talent working in contemporary culture, then that has to extend to designers and to having conversations about design. With Jeff, we've gotten to a point where the conversation is really seamless. Jeff understands what I'm trying to work toward and the aims of the Bemis organization as a whole. There's a lot of mutual respect, both in terms of what we're trying to achieve and in the kind of intellectual dialogue that gives rise to the work. It's been very fruitful on both ends.

out of Homasote, which is compressed paper, so it absorbs certain frequencies. Since we were creating this porous wall, we wanted to backlight it so the room could be softly lit during dance parties and evening events. The design sounds complex, but it's actually done simply. The center of the wall has a 12-foot radius going in one direction, and the two ends have 12-foot radii in the opposite direction. This creates a convex to concave to convex pattern, so the multicurved surface warps the sound. The ribs are made of plywood, which we cut ourselves. The wall probably cost less than $2,000, if you don't include the time and labor that we donated; yet it's an extremely functional component.

Initially the soft wall was only supposed to last for six months, but the team at the center liked it so much that they've decided to keep it. They use the space for all types of events. The center's symposium about architecture in the Midwest, which happens annually, has met there. There have been dance parties and experimental music concerts. People always think, "Oh my gosh, I'm moving to the Midwest; it's going to be horribly boring," but there's a powerful contemporary art scene in Omaha. There aren't very many galleries, but Bemis is at the center of the action. They do pretty radical exhibitions, so it's become a hub for this community.

We never really did pro bono work of this kind before, but it has become ▶

a big part of our practice since then. Our experience with Bemis showed us that we can actually do much more experimental work through these pro bono partnerships than we often can with our other clients.

My partner, E. B. Min, and I both have art backgrounds from before we went to architecture school, so we've always been very interested in contemporary art. Through this work, we've been able to forge long-term relationships and become true advisors to Bemis. At this point, I've actually been involved in the center longer than any of the staff, so I have a real base of knowledge about the facility.

Civic

39571 Project

39571 Project
Location Pass Christian, Mississippi **Date** 2006 **Client** Martha Murphy **Design firm** SHoP Architects
Design team Reese Campbell, Kimberly Holden, Federico Negro, Mark Ours, Gregg Pasquarelli,
Christopher Sharples, Coren Sharples, William Sharples **Area** 11,500 sq. ft. **Estimated value of pro bono**
design services Over $100,000 **Website** www.shoparc.com

Martha Murphy
Resident,
Pass Christian, Mississippi

CLIENT

The town where I live, Pass Christian, Mississippi, lost 100 percent of
its businesses and eight out of every ten houses during Hurricane Katrina.
We were obliterated, just wiped off the map. The first thing I realized
after the storm is that a community is not its buildings; a community is
something different and more. But the second thing I realized is that
buildings help define a community and they add dimension to its activities. SHoP's sense of community is what appealed to me when the
firm entered and won a national design competition for a Tulane University building project that I was involved with as a donor. The firm had
an interesting way of looking at problems as opportunities.

In Pass Christian, our world was down, and it seemed incredibly important to see something go up. To be a community, we needed a structure;
we needed a place to gather. Most immediately, we needed a place to
shelter the goods that were being donated from around the world. The
world was unfathomably generous; every organization you can think of
sent supplies, and we needed to find a way to disperse them.

It was enormously difficult for us to unload materials and deal with them
in a rational way. We got a load of lumber and passed it out to all the
people who needed it to repair their houses, but there was very little residents could do. You have to remember that people's hammers were
gone, their nails had washed away. And we were concerned about all the
new materials getting wet.

We were an unbelievably beleaguered people. Our resources were absolutely zilch. We were dependent on outside people with energy,
resources, and the will and the generosity of spirit to come help us. And
that is what SHoP did. Here were these amazing architects and engineers, people who build structures, helping us figure out where to get a
truck, where to unload boxes, where to put the contents of those boxes,
how to discard the boxes, and how to use the new materials. The architects were immensely empathetic without being all maudlin. They were
energetic without being kinetic. They were concerned. They were warm.
They were alert. They were creative. They were everything you could
possibly want people to be. ▹

William Sharples
Principal, SHoP Architects,
New York, New York

ARCHITECT

In the summer of 2005,
SHoP won a design com-
petition for a new build-
ing at Tulane University
in New Orleans. Through
the competition, we met
Martha Murphy. We were
scheduled to sign the
contracts for the project
the week after Hurricane
Katrina hit. Instead,
Martha called us from
her home in Mississippi
four or five days after
the storm and said, "I just
lost my whole town. The
only building standing
is the school. I need you to
come here and prove to
me that you can do every-
thing you said in the
interview—right here,
right now." So we did.

Two principals from
SHoP and an engineer
friend of ours from the
firm Buro Happold ▹

flew to Mississippi and basically camped out on site, where we started to work with local residents and the U.S. Army Corps of Engineers to set up a triage for the community. Together, in about three weeks, we erected a 6,000-square-foot tent to house medical, food, and other emergency supplies.

For Martha, the most important thing was to build an actual structure with a foundation and proper enclosure. So, in early October, we started designing a building, not even entirely clear on what it would be other than that it would mimic what the tent was already doing. Martha started to realize that with everything wiped out, we needed architecture to inspire and reinvigorate. It went from getting something up as quickly as possible to creating something that would be a place for the community to gather, not so much in the short term, but potentially for the next five or six years or more.

The building is really two separate enclosures joined by an outdoor canopy. The building to the east is associated with food, including a restaurant and grocery store. And the building to the west includes a bookstore, a beauty salon, and non-profit space. Martha felt we needed to bring some level of normalcy back. It was a balance between literally feeding the community and feeding its soul and culture.

The porch was the key. It created a canopy that tied everything together into ▶

On the back of an envelope, Bill Sharples sketched what would be a quick, easy, extremely functional, and durable building: a place to house goods and perform services and a way to be out of the weather. It was brilliantly designed and utterly simple. In this climate, it rains heavily, the air becomes very stale and stagnant, and things mildew, so the architects designed this lovely building that made use of the breeze. It faces south and has a big, tall ceiling that allows the heat to rise. It also has a huge porch, something that was, and is, important to many of us. After Katrina, that porch was a place for us to be a community.

One night, Reese Campbell and Federico Negro were up very late designing. They were being so careful, building on a shoestring budget, conscious of the lack of available materials and limited labor. But I asked, "If you could design anything you wanted—not needing to worry about the cost or the time and energy—what would it be?" They said, "The roof." Then they designed the most soaring, lyrical, magical roof ever. It is grand; it looks like whale bones or the ribs of a boat. People see all sorts of things in the roof.

I was extremely involved with the design. The place I love had just been obliterated. I loved the city's vernacular architecture, but I could not stand to see anything that would have been a replica of the past. It would have felt like Disneyland or something. But I love our new building. I love the tall ceilings and the life on the porch. It is very communal and casual, very elegant and graceful. A porch was exactly what we needed: A community needs contact; you need for your paths to cross. It was important to us to fortify ourselves as a community. We needed a sense of order in the chaos, and SHoP was a big part of making that process a rich, warm, and sustaining part of our life rather than a tragedy.

one clear moment. We wanted the porch itself to have a dramatic effect as you approached, so we focused on the underbelly latticework or the ribbing system. The porch was definitely something never seen before in that region in terms of what you could do with wood and metal. We used our digital capabilities at SHoP to come up with a technique that we could implement and that the local labor force could build easily. We put together a set of documents and spreadsheets based on assembly sequences. Everything was numbered, everything had its place; it was all laid out for the contractor, who was a Baptist minister who had only ever built 7-Eleven stores. In the end, it went together like clockwork.

When someone comes to you and says, "I need something immediately and it needs to deal with these issues," you focus on those issues. Our reaction to the situation in Mississippi was no different than to 9/11. On 9/11, a number of our staff went down to Ground Zero to volunteer. In the following days, Battery Park City representatives contacted us and said they needed a temporary pedestrian bridge built as quickly as possible. We developed the Rector Street Bridge within a matter of days, working with emergency services when the pile was still smoldering. Pro bono projects, like these, influence the culture of our office; there is no way you can put a value on it, but it clearly informs how we respond to general emergencies on regular projects. ▸

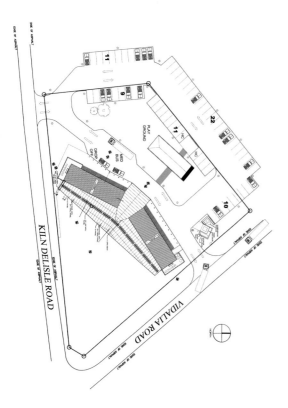

We responded immediately to Martha's needs; we did not think about it, we just did it. Things would have been different for us, obviously, if Martha had not caught us. We probably would have gone down there and worked with Tulane on some of the master planning projects. But once you get your hands into something as real as getting a community back on its feet, you just focus on that challenge. We felt like we were part of something big. We wanted to be there, and we would have done anything necessary to get the job done.

Food Chain

Urban Farming Food Chain
Location Los Angeles, California **Date** Begun 2008 **Client** Urban Farming **Client liaison** Joyce Lapinsky
Design firm Elmslie Osler Architect **Design team** Catherine Lowry, Robin Elmslie Osler **Area** Four gardens,
each 1,800 sq. ft. **Cost** Over $50,000 **Estimated value of pro bono design services** Over $100,000
Websites www.urbanfarming.org, www.eoarch.com

Robin Elmslie Osler
Principal, Elmslie Osler
Architect,
New York, New York

Joyce Lapinsky
Program Development Consultant, Urban Farming,
Los Angeles, California

ARCHITECT

The Urban Farming Food Chain project was the first time that my firm got involved in pro bono work. I was introduced by a mutual friend to Taja Sevelle, the head of Urban Farming, a national organization that plants food on unused land to feed the needy. She came to our office in Huntsville, Alabama, when we were working on an Anthropologie store with two very large green living walls that look like hanging carpets filled with sedum plants. At that time, we had a model of the store in the office. Taja asked, "Can you grow food on those walls?"

I found out that, yes, indeed, you could grow food using the same type of system. But if you just want to grow food on a wall, you don't really need an architect. I could have put her in contact with the manufacturer of the system. However, thinking about it more carefully, I realized that I could make the idea more ▶

CLIENT

Urban Farming seeks to make healthy foods more accessible to under-served, impoverished communities in the U.S. and around the world by planting food in unused spaces. Originally we wanted to create a garden on the rooftop of a partner organization in Los Angeles, but because the building was leased, we couldn't. Working with Robin Osler of Elmslie Osler Architect and George Irwin of Green Living Technologies, we began to consider vertical wall gardens as a way to serve the Los Angeles community. The wall idea expanded our opportunities and thus our ability to reach people. A food wall is also more ergonomically correct for gardeners; it is much more comfortable to stand and garden than to kneel on the ground.

We understood as we embarked on this project that we were, in a sense, pioneers. We asked for input from everyone because this wall was new for all of us. The idea of a food wall system itself is not new, but the way we branded the project was. We needed walls that had certain physical characteristics, including exposure to at least four hours of direct sunlight, access to water, and room for at least a foot of horizontal plant growth out from the wall.

We decided on doing four garden walls in Los Angeles's Skid Row, a place where people would greatly benefit from healthy food and hopefully feel empowered by the opportunity to learn new skills. Robin came up with the idea of creating a path to connect each of the locations. Like the gardens that our organization creates on the ground in vacant lots, we wanted the walls to be accessible to pedestrians. However, as Robin and I walked around downtown Los Angeles, we had to rethink this idea—it was evident that the sidewalks were homeless people's homes.

Though the path was not achievable, we remained committed to making the project identifiable. To do this, Robin conceived of and designed Guardian Wall Boxes. They are boxes made up of flat panels that ▶

THE ANNENBERG FOUNDATION
WEINGART CENTER ASSOCIATION

URBAN FARMING FOOD CHAIN

ELMSLIE OSLER
ARCHITECT

GREEN LIVING
TECHNOLOGIES

GREENHEART FARMS

MEYER TRUCKING

WINERY MUSIC
AWARDS

STEINBECK
VINEYARDS &
WINERY

CALIFORNIA POLYTECHNIC STATE UNIVERSITY
SAN LUIS OBISPO

SUSTAINABLE AGRICULTURE RESOURCE
CONSORTIUM

GREEN ACRES
LAVENDER
FARM

RENEE'S
GARDEN SEEDS

NATIONAL
GARDENING
ASSOCIATION

SEED SAVERS
EXCHANGE

FARM SUPPLY
COMPANY

UC DAVIS
COMMON
GROUND
GARDEN
PROGRAM

ATLANTIC RECORDS

compelling by designing a scheme to highlight the walls. So I put my head into writing the program, building on an idea based on Frederick Law Olmsted's Emerald Necklace and using terminology related to jewelry. The Emerald Necklace in Boston strung together a number of the city's most beautiful and prominent parks, connecting them via waterways and additional parkland. In our design, the wall gardens are the jewels of the necklace. Joyce Lapinsky at Urban Farming came up with the name that tied the idea together: Food Chain.

Los Angeles became our first pilot city with four projects centered downtown in Skid Row. Unfortunately, Skid Row is not a unique urban condition, though it is extreme. The neighborhood is filled with shelters, missions, and support services that tend to be big on canned food. Not to diminish the good work that those organizations are doing, but the residents of Skid Row are not eating healthy food, which has implications for a host of other issues, like their mental and physical health. Many people are dealing with addiction and other psychological problems, and proper nutrition can help them through those challenges.

During our search for sites for the gardens, we looked at parks and courtyards that closed at night. On Skid Row, the site has to close or it's a nightmare. As much as we would have liked to have the gardens located on the street, it was necessary to keep security in mind. ▶

The sites also needed appropriate access and south-southwest-facing light. As of today, four sites in the Food Chain have been built. One at Skid Row Housing Trust, which focuses on fighting homelessness, is in a back courtyard, visible once you enter the building. The Weingart Center Association, which houses homeless people, has a garden located in a fenced-in courtyard visible from the street. Not far from there, a third garden wall is located at the Los Angeles Regional Food Bank, and the wall's daily harvest is donated to the organization. The fourth site, Miguel Contreras Learning Complex, is a high school in downtown Los Angeles.

I attended the installation of the wall in the Weingart Center courtyard, where, through a partnership with California Polytechnic State University, San Luis Obispo, the walls had been "pregrown" with mature plants. There were fully grown lemons, strawberries, beans, and tomatillos. It was extraordinary. Hummingbirds and butterflies started to appear. I turned to a woman and said, "This is amazing! Look at the hummingbirds and the butterflies." She had never seen a butterfly or hummingbird on Skid Row. Never. The wall literally changed the ecosystem around the plants. People living in the shelter were full of pride putting the wall up; the energy was infectious and incredibly moving. I continue to do these kinds of projects because they truly impact individuals in the community. ▷

display the names of the sponsors and donors for each wall. Our default color for the boxes is a beautiful yellow with green showing through the lettering. Some of the boxes are hollow containers with lockable doors that are used to store garden supplies and materials right on the wall. Having the supplies stowed away and ready for use at any time is very convenient. The boxes finish the project and look great.

It took a good while to finish phase two—building the wall boxes—because we needed another round of funding. I am really glad it happened that way. It allowed us to live with the walls, understand them, and discover what we really needed. With more fund-raising, we hope phase three will include either portable or adjacent kitchens at all four food wall locations. There community members could cook the food we grow. They would be inspired to learn how to cook, get more involved with farming the walls, and could even sell the food. The kitchen will tie the project together.

One of our priorities is to train people to use the system. It's a constant need, as there is a lot to learn and people's commitment to the gardens change. Everyone—from the Urban Farming organization to those harvesting the healthy food to the individuals who receive it—benefits from a project like the Food Chain. Urban Farming seeks the inclusion of the community in these projects. These gardens, including the food walls, have become a hub and a meeting place that provides opportunities. Residents in the community who lack resources have met individuals in businesses, elected officials, and some of our nonprofit partners. Atlantic Records has even adopted Urban Farming as its charity, and its artists have visited our sites.

Urban Farming began in Detroit in 2005 with three gardens. Today it has grown to include 600 gardens around the world. Since there are more available walls with access to sun and water than there are rooftops, the Food Chain has expanded our opportunities to provide access to healthy foods. We look to continue to expand and teach people about different food sources through such projects.

A schoolteacher who had started a garden club at Miguel Contreras Learning Complex told me a story about a young boy who had never tasted a fresh tomato. The only tomatoes that he had ever seen had been at McDonald's, where he always took them off of his hamburger because he didn't know what they were and he didn't like the flavor. Excited after seeing his first tomato from the wall he exclaimed, "Oh, this is what a tomato looks like!" He wanted to eat it like an apple. He had no idea a tomato could taste so good, and he took it home to show his parents. The educational component is happening over time with help from the hosts who tend the walls. The gardens are truly changing lives.

Hollygrove

Hollygrove Market and Farm
Location New Orleans, Louisiana **Date** Master plan begun 2008; pavilion 2009 **Client** Carrollton-Hollygrove Community Development Corporation **Client liaison** Paul Baricos **Design firm** crgarchitecture **Design team** Ian Daniels, Nels Erickson, Dan Etheridge, Cordula Roser Gray, Joseph Kimbrell, Dominick Lang, Kimberly Lewis, Sam Richards, Joe Rodriguez, Jeff Schwartz, Emilie Taylor, Michael Visintainer, Seth Welty **Area** Master plan 40,000 sq. ft.; pavilion 800 sq. ft. **Cost** Master plan $750,000; pavilion $20,000 **Estimated value of pro bono design services** Master plan $50,000; pavilion $10,000 **Websites** www.hollygrovemarket.com, www.tulanecitycenter.org

Cordula Roser Gray
Principal, crgarchitecture,
New Orleans, Louisiana

ARCHITECT

The idea for the Hollygrove Market and Farm was to develop the site in a way that would teach people in the neighborhood about sustainability, educate them about healthy means of feeding themselves, create work opportunities, and support community businesses. The site is in one of many underprivileged neighborhoods in New Orleans. Even before the storm, the community faced socially challenging issues—unemployment, poverty, and a lack of educational opportunities.

Beyond the existing building and new pavilion, the master plan for the site includes planting beds and teaching areas, where people can learn about growing their own food and eating healthfully. The pavilion organizes the site. Placed near the entrance, it is visually accessible from Olive Street. To draw people in, we also placed a demonstration garden along the ▶

Paul Baricos
Executive Director, Carrollton-Hollygrove
Community Development Corporation,
New Orleans, Louisiana

CLIENT

After Hurricane Katrina, we formed the Carrollton-Hollygrove Community Development Corporation to help residents return to their homes in this neighborhood. About two years ago, we turned our focus to community revitalization as well as housing issues. We saw food justice and food security as an issue in Hollygrove, especially after the storm. There are several corner stores here, but they mostly sell alcohol, cigarettes, and junk food—nothing fresh.

We had 1 acre of ground and a building on the site, but we weren't quite sure what to do with them. So we approached Tulane City Center, an outreach arm of the university's School of Architecture that focuses on urban research and design, to develop a master plan for the site itself. In addition to making it a market and a training farm, we wanted it to be an education center that could teach about the sustainability of locally grown and organic food, food security, and green building. The master plan document that the team produced went a long way in helping us secure our initial grant to build the green pavilion.

The pavilion, built by the Tulane students under Cordula Roser Gray of crgarchitecture, is a shaded space for teaching. The structure serves as an example of environmentally conscious building and has become the centerpiece of the site. People immediately see the pavilion when they first come in. Its materials are brightly colored, and the roof is dramatic. A gutter runs prominently through the roof to collect rainwater and empties into a 1,000-gallon cistern enclosed in translucent Plexiglas. We're so proud of it; when we give tours or when we talk to anybody about the farm, the pavilion is the first thing we mention.

As far as the community is concerned, the garden is really exciting. Believe it or not, a lot of the adults in the area have never seen crops growing before. It's also an eye-opening experience for kids. The first Saturday of every month, we put on workshops and activities to introduce kids to gardening, growing, and cooking. They find it fascinating. ▶

street. We want the site to offer people a place to gather, communicate, and learn from each other. It is open to the community all day and signs explain everything that is going on. The agenda is to provide regionally grown produce to sell in the Saturday market. The existing building is currently undergoing extensive renovations; the ground floor will become an enclosed indoor market, which is already partially operating.

The pavilion was originally in the last phase of the master plan, but it became the first thing we were able to realize because *Home & Garden* magazine (of the *Times Picayune*) and the Aveeno company donated money specifically for a pavilion and water-catchment system. I led a design/build class at Tulane University with a group of students through Tulane City Center, which runs applied urban research and outreach programs at the School of Architecture. We had the task of designing and building the pavilion in about two and a half months, so it would be ready when the donors visited the city.

The Tulane City Center offers opportunities for faculty and students from Tulane's School of Architecture to be engaged in projects with real contextual challenges. The City Center is involved in a wide range of partnerships with a variety of different community-based organizations. Due to the reputation that it has built over the past few years, organizations routinely approach me about it, ▸

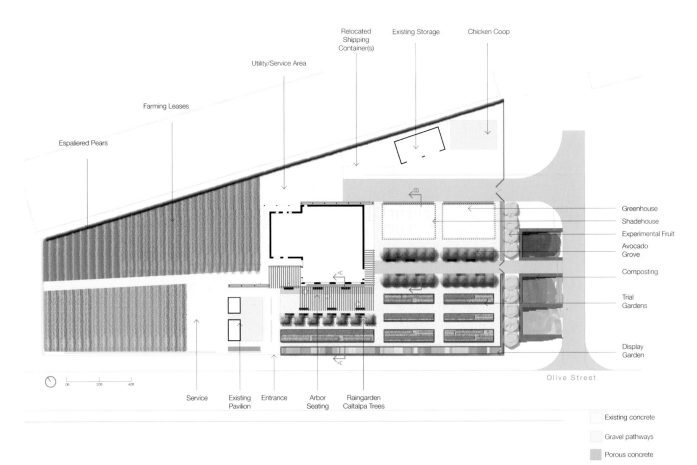

Espaliered Pears
Farming Leases
Utility/Service Area
Relocated Shipping Container(s)
Existing Storage
Chicken Coop

Greenhouse
Shadehouse
Experimental Fruit
Avocado Grove
Composting
Trial Gardens
Display Garden

Olive Street

Service
Existing Pavilion
Entrance
Arbor Seating
Raingarden Caltalpa Trees

Existing concrete
Gravel pathways
Porous concrete

The Power of Pro Bono

since I am an adjunct faculty member of the School of Architecture. We then work with clients to understand their needs and develop strategies to realize their projects.

The work that the City Center and other architects, like myself, do must be affordable and work within social and economical constraints, but it also has to have a lot of potential. Hollygrove's food center helps spread an educational agenda and also creates a cornerstone that people can use as a gathering point. Many reconstruction projects in the city have been successful at the neighborhood level because people have come together and organized themselves. Any community-based structure or organization needs a place where people can come to talk to each other and with which they can identify themselves. If we can create a multitude of those, they can bring the city together again. Anything from a design and, more important, build point of view that can lift the city up is a positive issue that we as architects should be engaged in.

The farm has become valuable for training residents who are interested in organic urban farming, as well as being a source for some of the produce sold in the market. Each week, we purchase about $4,000 in produce from the farm for the market, and we think we can triple that eventually. About 15 percent of the food we buy is from urban growers, and the rest is from farms within 100 miles of the city. The farmers now have confidence that they can sell their produce straight to us. They're expanding their crops because they know they have a place to sell them.

At the beginning of the process, we hadn't decided on a name for the market, and we were tossing a lot of things around. Someone suggested "Hollygrove Market and Farm," and, due to the neighborhood's reputation before the storm, some community members said, "If you use the name Hollygrove, you will turn some people off." But that's really why we're here; we're working to change that reality, and, of course, that perception. These days, others refer to us as the farmers' market, and all the time, people in the neighborhood say, "It's not the farmers' market; it's the Hollygrove market!" It's something the Hollygrove community is really proud of.

P-Patch

Interbay P-Patch Garden Hub
Location Seattle, Washington **Date** 2008 **Client** Interbay P-Patch **Client liaison** Ray Schutte **Design firm** CAST Architecture **Design team** Stefan Hampden, Matt Hutchins, Nathan Walker **Area** 800 sq. ft. **Cost** $12,000 **Estimated value of pro bono design services** $16,700 **Website** www.castarchitecture.com

Ray Schutte
Chair, Interbay P-Patch Leadership Team,
Seattle, Washington

CLIENT

The Interbay P-Patch is made up of seventy plots of land that residents can lease for personal gardening. So it's a place where people come together. CAST Architecture has done three projects for our community garden: The first was building the toolshed and kitchen; the second was the grape arbor that extends off the toolshed; and third was the kiosk. The architectural elements of each structure visually connect them; that cohesiveness is pretty unusual for a community garden. We are fortunate to have this relationship with CAST, and it all started in 2002, when Nathan Walker, a principal at the firm at that time, had a garden plot at the P-Patch, and we started talking about replacing our toolshed.

The toolshed was a tiny, old building that held gardening implements, as well as a propane stove so the structure could also serve as a kitchen. The building was in the garden's central courtyard, and it wasn't very functional. The city of Seattle has a Neighborhood Matching Fund that gives local organizations money for projects that enhance the city. The dollar amount given is then matched by volunteer work hours, donated money, or resources from people in the community. Through the fund, we got a grant of $12,000 to build the new structure.

The terms of the grant require a good deal of community involvement, so we got the garden members together to discuss the design for the new structure, and CAST facilitated that meeting. I've never seen so many people participate in a community activity. The meeting generated many ideas. One of the most important questions raised was about the placement of the building. Another concern was that the garden be more accessible to wheelchairs.

CAST came back with several different ideas. Our steering committee picked up on one of the firm's proposals, and the designers presented it back to the group. The garden community had suggestions about what was missing, and CAST incorporated several of these ideas. The architects surprised everybody with the design for the shed. First of all, it was bigger than we expected. They expanded the building so that the kitchen and toolshed are separated. A breezeway connects the two areas, ▷

Matt Hutchins
Principal, CAST
Architecture,
Seattle, Washington

ARCHITECT

One of our firm's original principals, Nathan Walker, was a gardener at the Interbay P-Patch. By virtue of having a plot there, he became familiar with the needs and goals of the community. Part of the garden's core mission is to bring people together, and while it was successful in doing that, those activities didn't really have a home; they happened ad hoc. Basically, they had substandard facilities and outstanding community spirit. We wanted to support the sense of community by providing space for the gardeners to enact their mission.

We began by surveying the garden members. Their steering committee laid out the basic parameters, and we developed the design for the new shed around the feedback we got from them and Nathan. There were immense limits on the budget, but no limitations on motivation or ambition, so we stuck with it and made it work. In the end, we weren't able to build 100 percent consensus among the garden members, but after the shed was built, the naysayers conveniently disappeared. ▷

There are two functional aspects of the design of the shed—the storage box and the community box. The storage box houses the tools. The goal of the community box was to be the centerpiece for whatever activity was going on in the garden, the space where the community comes together. We wanted the structure to provide a safe place where you can swing the doors open and use the kitchen to host potlucks. The translucent roof bridges the two structures and forms a portico, kind of like a big porch or stage for local happenings.

The shed fosters all kinds of activities; people can get out of the weather and still come to the garden, hang out with folks, and enjoy both being outside and being with other people. The community has such a strong connection to the space that it has become a hub. Until we built it, we always referred to the project as "a shed," and as soon as we finished it, people started calling it "the community center."

Last year, we built new signage for the garden's entrance. Each new piece of the Interbay P-Patch brings the message of the benefits of community gardening to more people. The increased interest led to us build an information kiosk, where visitors can learn about the program and gardeners can find out about events. Another fun project for us was the grape arbor, which gathers rainwater off of the concave tool-shed roof and pours it through the center of the kiosk on a rain chain. ▸

allowing air to move through the structure. On a hot summer day, it's rather nice. The design also provided some shelter from the rain. It's amazing how many people you can cram into a little space when you need to.

To build the structure, we scheduled construction parties for volunteers. One day, sixty of our 120 members showed up. It was incredible, and the CAST employees were there wearing tool belts and overalls, building with us. The team supervised the drilling of every hole and the placing of every screw that holds down the galvanized tin.

After the structure was complete, there was a lot more interest in the garden, and we had more visitors coming through the space. Given that, we wanted to build a kiosk with a board where we could post notices about events and explain our history. CAST came up with the idea of etching our history into the glass. From far away, you can see through it, but up close, you can read the etchings. Both sides of the kiosk have a panel: one for official garden news and the other for community happenings.

These projects have aged really well. The gardeners tend the communal space and bring a high level of care to it. None of the garden's architectural elements have ever been tagged with graffiti, which I think is because when something is well designed, it creates a presence that taggers respect.

Our garden has helped broaden awareness of community gardens as a whole. The architectural elements give our gardeners a sense of belonging and our visitors the feeling of arriving at a true destination. That, in my mind, is what architecture is all about.

When people see the P-Patch, it plants a seed, and they often go on to participate in or start a community garden of their own.

In pro bono work, you need to set clear limits, because it's very easy for projects to get out of control. Once you're freed from a traditional client and budget, you want to do the coolest stuff that you possibly can, but the reality is that there's only so much time that you can invest. The key for any pro bono project is that whoever is in charge be really committed to the cause. You have to love the project in order to get through the rough times. Compared to other work, we've been trying to keep the firm's pro bono jobs relatively small so that they can be managed and executed by a single person.

As architects, the main benefits we get from pro bono work are certainly not tangible, but one thing that has been wonderful is that, ever since we did the original shed, a gardener from the P-Patch periodically drops by the office with fresh vegetables or fruit. The members have been thanking us for years. Each time that gift arrives is a moment when we realize that we did a really good thing.

Randall Overlook

Randall Museum Overlook
Location San Francisco, California **Date** 2008 **Client** Randall Museum **Client liaison** Chris Boettcher
Design firm EHDD **Design team** Marc L'Italien, Matthew Rouse **Area** 600 sq. ft. **Cost** $40,000 **Estimated value of pro bono design services** $10,000 **Websites** www.randallmuseum.org, www.ehdd.com

Chris Boettcher
Executive Director, Randall Museum,
San Francisco, California

CLIENT

The Randall Museum is an interactive natural history museum for children, named in honor of a remarkable woman, the late Josephine D. Randall. Through Ms. Randall's hard work, the museum was established in 1937, and we acquired our current building in 1951. We have a site with an amazing view of all of San Francisco, and we had long wanted to build a bench near the overlook point. As I explained to architect Marc L'Italien during a workshop that he attended at the museum, there had been discussions of buying either prefabricated benches or an off-the-shelf outdoor seating area for the site. I told Marc about the plan, and EHDD decided to make the project the focus of an in-house design competition, whose program Marc and I wrote together. I told the firm what we were looking for and provided some site drawings, and off we went.

We wanted a place where people could sit and look at the city, have a picnic for the day, or watch the stars at night. Most of all, we wanted the design to be special; we didn't want it to be just a few benches sitting here. We could have done that, and it might have been a lot cheaper, but we wanted to have something that was more architectural and unique. Protecting the view for visitors higher up on our site was a priority as well, so this led us to choose a design that was very uninvasive.

A number of people from EHDD came to the museum to look at drawings of the site and take pictures, and in the end, seven members of the firm participated in the competition. Every single entrant approached the site differently, but we chose Matt Rouse because his idea fit the program the best. What is nice about Matt's design is that you can sit and look at either the city view or the museum. We sometimes have large public events here. We also have camps in the summer and school groups that drop in, and we wanted to allow people to all sit relatively close together. ▸

Marc L'Italien
Principal, EHDD,
San Francisco, California

ARCHITECT

I was taking a woodworking class at the Randall Museum, and one of the instructors, Chris Boettcher, also happened to be the museum's director. When I told him that I was an architect, he described an idea he had to build a seating area to take advantage of the view of San Francisco from the property. I said, "You know, that's an interesting idea. What would you think about a design competition?" His eyes lit up.

The timing was serendipitous because EHDD was getting ready to celebrate its sixtieth anniversary. Rather than throwing a party or having an exhibit of our work, we thought we should give something back. We wanted to do something that would use our expertise, exercise the young talent in the office, and give a client in need something worthwhile. At the time, our idea was just for EHDD to generate a design that fit these parameters, but our involvement in the Randall Museum project turned out to be much more than that.

Seven of our employees ended up submitting designs for a seating area for the museum. The solutions ranged from very pragmatic to more sculptural pieces. Overall, Matt Rouse's scheme had a little bit of everything. He was inspired by both the program and the site, ▸

We had some money for the project from our board of directors, and then we applied for matching money from San Francisco's Community Challenge Grant Program, which really helped make the project happen. The firm did all the design work pro bono and some of the staff volunteered to build the bench. We had work parties during which Matt and others from EHDD would help us mill the wood. All the woodworking was carried out here at the museum, while the metalwork was done by a company in the Bayshore District of San Francisco. We paid for that, along with the work to level the site.

The wood for the bench was reclaimed from a huge water tank in Santa Rosa, California. All the lumber had been salvaged and stacked in a lumberyard there. We completely remilled it and cut it into sections. Looking at the finished product, you can't tell that the wood is reused, but we feel that the fact that the bench is made out of all reclaimed materials echoes the museum's mission.

From beginning to end, this process took approximately six months; construction lasted about a month and the rest of the time was devoted to securing the funding and finalizing the design. Since its completion, the bench has seen endless use. Students on school field trips eat lunch here almost every day if the weather is good.

We are still in close touch with EHDD. I just talked to Matt the other day about a waterfall design we have in mind for our entryway. I was an architect before I started my career here, and I often wish I had known about EHDD then; it seems like a wonderful place to work. It's rare that junior members of a firm get a chance to compete for and run their own projects. I think the design competition reinvigorates the young architects, and we are really thankful for the work they've done here.

which has incredible cypress trees and a panoramic view of the city. It's really spectacular. Matt did something that nobody else did: He broke the rules. He actually extended his design out beyond the trees, which wasn't written into the program. That was a pretty profound move on his part. By looking at the desire lines and wear patterns in the grass, he discovered that people tend to congregate where it's sunny. Given that, he put the end of the seating and a table in the sunny area, but the bench starts within the designated site space. It's a very functional piece, yet it looks sculptural.

We knew we could never build the whole thing that Matt had designed with only the museum's budget, so its staff applied for a matching grant from the city of San Francisco, which doubled the amount of money available. A lot of the budget went toward leveling the site, and there was some metalwork for the bench's substructure that needed to be fabricated by a specialty shop. We worked with the Randall Museum to find the right fabricators for the job. Chris acquired both raw reclaimed redwood and rough-sawn salvaged redwood and brought it to the museum. We helped plane and finish mill it. Once it was milled, some of our staff worked alongside museum members and other volunteers to help install it. The construction was a combination of work done in the shop and on site. It was rewarding to be involved in the actual making of the bench. ▸

The overlook has become much more than a place to sit and have a sandwich. It's a place where teachers can engage classes while they take in the greater environment of the Bay Area. It allows the Randall Museum to have this incredible outdoor classroom right on the precipice of a hill with a striking view of the city. The museum never really had taken full advantage of that space before. For people who aren't at all engaged in the museum and just happen to stumble upon the site, they get to see something inspirational. It's a quiet piece in that it doesn't jump out at you, but its uniqueness is something that somebody might discover, which we think is really appealing.

It's been rewarding to be part of something that's special for a community. We like to go back and see how our projects age. Sometimes you see things that you didn't expect in terms of how people use buildings and make them their own. At the Randall Museum, for example, Matt designed the table to jut out so that it is accessible to those with disabilities, but the staff now call that area "the diving board" because little kids like to run up there and have their moms catch them when they get to the end. It doesn't get much better than that.

Roosevelt Park

Roosevelt Park Master Plan
Location Detroit, Michigan **Date** Begun 2008 **Client** Greater Corktown Development Corporation
Client liaison Meghan McEwen **Design firm** uRbanDetail **Design team** Phillip Cooley, Melissa Dittmer,
Tadd Heidgerken, Noah Resnick, Ryan Schirmang **Area** 360,000 sq. ft. **Cost** Phase one, $300,000;
estimated total, $5 million **Estimated value of pro bono design services** $56,000 to date **Websites**
www.corktowndetroit.org, www.urban-detail.com

Noah Resnick
Principal, uRbanDetail,
Detroit, Michigan

Meghan McEwen
Resident,
Detroit, Michigan

CLIENT

The Roosevelt Park project began when a collective, organized by uRbanDetail, circulated a questionnaire to residents and business owners in the Corktown neighborhood of Detroit. At that time, the park was, in essence, just an open space on a busy street. It was not at all quaint. The survey asked us if we would use the park, what we wanted from a public space, what we had we seen in other cities that inspired us, and other such questions.

I took the questionnaire very seriously. I spent a lot of time thinking about how the park would impact our lives. I have two small kids, so I really wanted a space that would not just be aesthetically pleasing but would also be functional. I wanted my kids to be able to play there. My family came from Chicago, so I was using Millennium Park as a benchmark. There is a lot of outdoor sculpture in Millennium Park; it's not just to look at, it is to use. So that was my directive: I wanted everything in the park to be functional.

As a design was formalized and construction of the first phase began, it was amazing to see how many people volunteered their time. You could drive or walk by on a weekend and there would be more than fifty people out there working. It was really exciting. Volunteers had the opportunity to pick up a shovel and get their hands in the earth. We were all able to be part of the project; it was something that we built together.

The site is immediately adjacent to an old, abandoned train station, which is a huge part of Roosevelt Park. The building is owned by a private individual, and the city wants him to tear it down. He doesn't want to spend the money to do that or to fix it up. But many people in Detroit love it because it's such an icon. We hope that our project will help save the building, but uRbanDetail has gone to great lengths to ensure that its design for the space will still work if the station is gone.

I can't stress enough how big this is for the neighborhood and the city in terms of morale. I personally feel an overwhelming sense of hope. To see so many people working in the park, in front of a beautiful ruin like the train station, which so many people had given up on, is extraordinary. ▸

ARCHITECT

When this all began, Roosevelt Park was just a huge plot of grass that wasn't even mowed regularly. An opportunity presented itself when Daimler Financial, which is headquartered in Detroit, offered to do a one-day cleanup of the park. A group of us immediately got involved. We said, "Let's do something more; let's try to turn this park into something incredible." We created a master plan to garner some interest, and Daimler Financial pledged $10,000 to get us started.

A group of six of us, local designers and friends, formed a collaborative. We looked at the site history, development economics, potential uses for the space, and the relationship of the park to the adjacent train station, which is a local icon. We wrote a basic programming survey to get the community involved. We distributed it to Corktown residents and people in metro and suburban Detroit to see what would bring them into this neighborhood. ▸

Historically, there has been a large homeless population in this park, and that made many residents wary. However, we made it very clear among ourselves that we were not going to force the homeless people to leave because of this revitalization. We were going to be sensitive to them as community members, so we gave them surveys to make sure they still had a place they could use. We also addressed the homeless by stepping outside the boundaries of the park and working with some of the nearby soup kitchens and local churches. Some of the homeless gentlemen volunteered as builders. They were happy to lend their time and work and to be included in the process.

The multiphase program was informed by the survey responses, which told us the community wanted typical things found in city parks, like basketball courts, skateboarding, soccer, and music. In the first phase, we began by beautifying the space. We created a concrete island with landscaping, which we built with the funds from Daimler Financial. When we showed the people at Daimler what we had done, they liked it so much that they said, "Great, here's $30,000 to do the next piece." So that's what we did this past summer. Now we're going to take the images of our most recent work back to Daimler and show our success in hopes of funding the next phase: a skate park. The idea is that each phase completed will help raise funds for the next. So far it has worked pretty well. ▶

One of the challenges of this project was basing the design on donated materials and equipment. Even though the city has pledged zero dollars to help us get this done, it has said we can do whatever we want there and has also donated materials. For example, the city had tons of huge granite slabs from an old park. There are now three central squares made up of the twenty-eight donated slabs. The idea is that they will be viewing platforms from which people can photograph the train station.

We've also built relationships with local urban-farming groups; we gave them extra topsoil, and they come and help us take care of our new plants. There is a barter system of sorts between different community groups.

For the most part, the labor has been all-volunteer. We only paid for the skilled labor required for welding the COR-TEN steel landscape planter walls. The big machines that we used, like the front-end loaders, were loaned to us free of charge by Michigan Forklift. Often people came to the site to photograph the train station, and then they would see us working and ask what we were doing. We'd tell them and they would offer to help, so we built a network that way. Friends, neighbors, and some of my students from the University of Detroit at Mercy helped out as well. It was really incredible. ▷

The thing about Detroit is that amazing opportunities like Roosevelt Park present themselves all the time. If I had stayed in New York or Cambridge, where I went to school, it would be fifteen years before I could actually design and build a park in the middle of the city, if I ever got the opportunity. It definitely would never happen before reaching forty. But in Detroit you can do that. Things happen in Detroit, and it's why people like myself, my wife, and our collaborators came here.

There are a lot of people here, including me, who believe the train station is utterly beautiful as it is, as an urban ruin. Roosevelt Park now celebrates and honors that beauty, providing a functional space for people who enjoy being in its shadow. It's a major victory for those who think the station shouldn't go anywhere. It makes people believe they can go to the park and that it is not just a place for the homeless to congregate.

Many of us in the neighborhood had been using the park for a long time, but this project is not just a rogue group of thirty-year-olds playing bocce ball in the field. Roosevelt Park now provides an outdoor community center of sorts; it's a place to play soccer, skateboard, listen to music, hang out, and relax. It is aesthetically pleasing, but more than that, it is something that residents of Corktown and all of Detroit are proud of. We live in a city where everyone talks about things falling down, and now there is the hope of creating something new and beautiful again.

Most nights during construction, my family walked to the park in the early evening, and a handful of the construction workers were driving forklifts and pushing huge piles of dirt. Our son was fascinated. He's three and a half, an age where he can really remember. He'll be able to enjoy the park long after it is finished, but I don't think he will ever forget those nights when we watched it all come together.

Community

Alvar Street
New Orleans, Louisiana
Meyer, Scherer &
Rockcastle

Goodwill
San Francisco,
California
McCall Design Group

Hands On
Atlanta, Georgia
Jova/Daniels/Busby

Kam Liu
Chicago, Illinois
Studio Gang Architects

Lavezzorio
Chicago, Illinois
Studio Gang Architects

Yawkey
Boston, Massachusetts
Chan Krieger NBBJ

Alvar Street

Alvar Street Branch Library
Location New Orleans, Louisiana **Date** 2006 **Client** New Orleans Public Library **Client liaison** Rica Trigs
Design firm Meyer, Scherer & Rockcastle **Design team** Leanne Larson, Paul Mellblom, Jeffrey Scherer
Area 2,250 sq. ft. **Cost** $800,000 **Estimated value of pro bono design services** $61,500 **Websites**
www.nutrias.org, www.msrltd.com

Rica Trigs
COO, New Orleans Public Library,
New Orleans, Louisiana

Jeffrey Scherer
Principal and CEO, Meyer,
Scherer & Rockcastle,
Minneapolis, Minnesota

CLIENT

The Alvar Street Branch Library is located in the Bywater neighborhood of the Lower Ninth Ward in New Orleans. Being below the floodplain, the building suffered severe and extensive water damage during Hurricane Katrina. The outside fared well, but the inside was entirely flooded, and almost all of the books were destroyed.

In the wake of the disaster, several groups approached the New Orleans Public Library with offers to help us rebuild, among them the American Library Association (ALA) and the *Library Journal*. The ALA also made a decision shortly after the storm to keep its prior commitment to the city and host its annual conference in New Orleans; it was the first major conference in the area post-Katrina. It was the *Library Journal*, however, that really came up with the idea for what was essentially an "Extreme Makeover, Library Edition."

We were introduced to architect Jeffrey Scherer of Meyer, Scherer & Rockcastle (MS&R) by way of the *Library Journal*. We engaged Jeffrey's services because we needed his expertise in library design. New Orleans had built its last library thirty years earlier, and no one on our staff was around at that time. Given the opportunity, we didn't want to just rebuild what we had; we wanted to rebuild smartly and give the citizens more, particularly in this area of the city, which so desperately needed our services.

The biggest challenge of this project was coordination. Everyone we dealt with, besides the contractors, was from out of town. We let the architects do their thing because we trusted them as library-design professionals. Even the initial vision that MS&R had for the space was very much in line with what we wanted and needed. As users, we tweaked the design—including the types of spaces and details such as shelving configurations—based on our knowledge of the community's needs. ▸

ARCHITECT

Like so many others, MS&R wanted to do something to help after Hurricane Katrina ravaged New Orleans. We quickly found an opportunity to lead the restoration and redesign of a branch library in the Ninth Ward. The New Orleans Public Library was in dire straits, and the citizens of New Orleans were desperate for their libraries to reopen, particularly since Internet access was so crucial in the early days post-Katrina. Our firm has designed and restored a significant number of libraries throughout our history, so the Alvar Street Branch Library was an obvious choice.

The library is housed in a Works Progress Administration building with good bones and a simple form, including high windows on the long flanking sides. Aesthetically, we didn't need to do anything to the exterior except clean, repaint, and relandscape. ▸

The inside was another story. The entire interior needed to be gutted, and most of the books had to be replaced due to water damage. We discovered that the building had its original 1930s built-in wood shelving along the exterior walls, which immediately posed a significant opportunity or dilemma: Should we refinish the wood shelving and save it? Or should we replace it with new metal shelving to save money? We saved it.

We knew right off the bat that our design had to fit into rigid economic constraints; we didn't have a blank check. The library also looked to our firm to help raise money. The national focus on post-Katrina New Orleans created a heightened awareness of the need. The empathetic atmosphere among donors and vendors made our job a lot easier. Vendors sent us lists of excess inventory that we could work with, and it was a win-win situation, since manufacturers receive tax write-offs for their material donations, as well as an opportunity to showcase their products and demonstrate their community spirit. One interesting thing about the inertia on the donation side is that there's a sort of one-upmanship among competitors, which can work in your favor on a project like this.

Our limited budget led to an innovative idea for the bookcase end panels. We worked with our shelving manufacturer to create new panels using sanded Plexiglas, which lets in more light. The panels ▸

became ideal canvases for graphics, and a local company donated its services to silk-screen onto them images of jazz musicians—including the Neville Brothers, Louis Armstrong, and Bessie Smith, who all went to school down the street. With more money, we may not have made those decisions, and I think the library would be the lesser for it.

Realizing the library may eventually flood again due to its location, we approached another manufacturer and got rubber flooring donated. Our firm had specified over 1 million square feet of the company's product over the past decade, so its owners were good to us. Our client assumed we would install carpet that ▶

would be thrown away in the next flood. Now they can just squeegee the water out without having to move everything outside and back in, saving time and resources. The constraint of being below the floodplain was addressed, at least in part, by using an alternate material.

Throughout the process, we had residents, the library board, vendors from around the country, and people in multiple states all focused on making this project happen. At the end of the day, it was impossible to ascribe a single author to any one thing. We removed ego from the equation. That spirit translates to all of MS&R's business; our employees and the vendors we work with remember what it feels like to do good, particularly when the results are so positive.

The Alvar Street Branch Library is full every day. The community members took it upon themselves to restore an overgrown park next door that dates back to the 1940s, and it's now a nice space for outdoor reading. Best of all, people around the city are seeing the benefits, showing their support, and working to get libraries for their neighborhoods.

Upon completion of the project, MS&R was hired to design a master plan for rebuilding the entire New Orleans Public Library system. We garnered a high level of trust because we had been so involved with the Alvar Street Branch Library. The residents were willing to listen to us and offer their own thoughts ▶

about where libraries should be in their communities. If we hadn't worked on the Alvar project, we probably wouldn't have had the success we had with the master plan. The New Orleans Public Library got $38 million appropriated—from a combination of private, public, and FEMA money—and is now closely following our plan.

The neighborhood embraced this project from the very beginning. Residents volunteered to remove damaged books and debris. It was an important effort because the community had no other real public infrastructure at the time. We were the first of the libraries—of any public city building, really—to come back online after Hurricane Katrina. Here was a job we could wrap our arms around and truly feel that progress was being made.

The library now is a quaint place, and the design suits the Bywater community. After the reconstruction was completed, community members went further, landscaping the grounds, which they continue to maintain, and shaping the book collection, which is now heavier on arts and culture. Even more so than before, the residents have a vested interest in the space. All of the programs are very well attended. We have extended the hours because of the use, and we even have tour groups that visit.

MS&R has been instrumental in reviving the Alvar Street Branch, as well as in envisioning the future of the greater New Orleans Public Library system. With the firm's help, one of the things we have incorporated into our master plan is "after-hours zones," which means our buildings must be able to accommodate different uses throughout the day and evening. At the Alvar Street Branch, we hold art nights, poetry readings, and other activities that the community coordinates with the branch manager, who is active in the greater library system as an advocate for her neighborhood. Similarly, the president of the Bywater Neighborhood Association has become a huge supporter of the library and even organized a festival there. This project helped us become what we wanted to be: a community hub.

Additionally, we have evolved the role of the New Orleans Public Library to serve as recovery central every time there is a disaster in the city. People can come in to get information about FEMA, the FDA, and hurricane preparedness. On the other extreme, we've also become a social gathering place. Yet in the middle of it all, we remain a library, here to provide resources. The Alvar Street Library was a successful pilot project that helped us redefine ourselves within the community.

Goodwill

Goodwill Fillmore Street Store

Location San Francisco, California **Date** 2007 **Client** Goodwill Industries of San Francisco **Client liaison** Lisa Zimmerman, director of marketing and communications **Design firm** McCall Design Group **Design team** John Chan, Mike McCall, Jeffrey Shiozaki **Area** 3,000 sq. ft. **Estimated value of pro bono design services** $32,000 **Websites** www.goodwill.org, www.mccalldesign.com

Mike McCall
Principal, McCall Design Group,
San Francisco, California

ARCHITECT

Goodwill, like every other entity that does merchandising, has some strong ideas when it comes to how its stores operate. It has a structure, but you sometimes can't really tell because the group's approach seems to be to pile as much stuff as possible into a space, which is kind of the thrift-store sensibility.

When I did a walk-through of an existing store early on, I discovered that Goodwill did a really good job with a lot of things, but they had challenges with others. From the beginning, we focused on making it easier for the customer to navigate the store. We did so by making the flow from department to department very logical. We also worked with certain elements of the décor to strengthen brand identity—Goodwill as a retail experience as opposed to just a thrift store.

You might think that people simply drop stuff off at the store and then it goes up for sale, but that's not the case. It's a very complex operation: Merchandise is dropped off, and then it needs to be staged, packed, and shipped downtown to a sorting facility. Once there, it is ordered, sized, and distributed to all different stores. We treated shipping and receiving ▶

Rachael Grossman
Chief of Organizational Advancement,
Goodwill Industries of San Francisco,
San Francisco, California

CLIENT

Goodwill Industries of San Francisco is part of a network of over 180 independent Goodwill stores and centers in North America. When we started to work with the McCall Design Group, in early 2007, our board of directors was wrestling with how to work with not only individuals but also communities in a systemic way to try to tackle the roots of poverty. One thing we knew for sure—and that we wanted McCall's help to realize—was that environmental stewardship should be a key component of our efforts.

We want people to associate Goodwill with environmental stewardship to the point that they have a trash bin, a recycling bin, and a Goodwill bin. We are even further along with that thinking now than when we were working with McCall. We selected the firm because of its strong environmental sensibility and retail expertise, so its staff could help us figure out how to use the store to drive mission awareness.

In terms of its design, the Fillmore Street store is open, bright, engaging, accessible, and lively. We really appreciate all the work McCall did, as our goal is to have this be a model for our other locations. We are trying to change the look and feel of our Goodwill stores—starting with this one—so they are of interest to a whole new type of shopper. We have a merchandiser who does window displays at the Fillmore Street store. We are trying to make it as compelling as possible for the area, which is an interesting one as it borders the largely working class Western Addition and the very high-end Pacific Heights neighborhoods.

To draw people into the store, we created a 70-foot photographic mural, which has portraits of donors and shoppers. These are real people who shop, donate, and are part of the Fillmore community. We talked at length about a painted mural but decided we wanted to highlight real people. We also felt it dusted off our image and showed that it could be hip to buy Goodwill. ▶

the way we would have with a normal retailer. It's not very complex stuff, but if you don't do it, it really messes up your day-to-day operations.

I think that there's a nice market for secondhand merchandise now. It's not just about being environmentally sensitive; it's about being socially sensitive. We wanted to make the Fillmore Street store coherent and shoppable. If that is where a family can afford to shop, why shouldn't that experience be manageable, convenient, and even fun? There's no reason for it to look junky, dirty, and crowded. It should be organized and fashion-forward.

One of the things I liked about working with Goodwill is that we worked with everybody. It was an opportunity to totally immerse ourselves in the organization. When we work with fashion retailers, as we often do, they have their whole organizations, and we get into them in a way that's sometimes a little bit like cogs in a machine. We deal with good people, but we don't really get exposure to the whole organization. With Goodwill, everybody is considered to be sort of like family.

For me, the partnership was fruitful. There's no pretense with Goodwill. They are who they are, and the organization is what it's about. But underneath the retail, Goodwill is all about job training for people who have never been able to hold down a job. There's a low success rate but a high degree of reward when things do ▶

The McCall team helped us design a donation facility that is attached to the store but has a separate entrance, allowing people to quickly and easily drop off their items. The idea is also to draw them into the store to shop. As a result, we have dramatically increased the amount and quality of our material donations, which are our lifeblood. The success of the Fillmore Street store has inspired us to look at relocating some of our other stores that have leases coming due in the next year, so we can incorporate more robust donation capacities in those facilities.

We have a job-training program in certain stores throughout the country, and the Fillmore location is one of those sites. The program focuses on training all levels of employees from entry level to management. It teaches new employees both how to work and how to work in retail.

We are in the process of changing some elements of our corporate culture to support a more streamlined design process. We are also starting to make decisions with more of a focus on our customers' needs. Goodwill is used to getting donations and pushing the merchandise through our stores, but we are trying to optimize value now, not unlike other traditional retailers. It requires that we develop a much more customer-driven approach in everything we do. It is a big change, and it affects every part of our organization.

What we loved about the architects at McCall is that they thought conceptually and they were very taken by our mission. They brought a lot of creative ideas to programming the space and making it a holistic part of our services. I know that McCall is interested in continuing to work with us, and we would like to keep working with them. We are committed to upgrading the look, feel, and branding of our stores.

work out. To participate in that is extremely fulfilling. That's what makes pro bono work fun to do; you're exposed to the mission and vision of the organization at a very fundamental level. The job training is the real crux of the mission for Goodwill.

We structured the project the same way we would a billable job. I didn't know how else to do it; I guess it's that simple. With every project, we build our management, administrative procedures, and processes, and we hope they're efficient. We kept track of all the same things: time, materials, reimbursables, etc.

We have used Goodwill in our portfolio, not because it was pro bono, but because of the design. It really resonated with one client who thought its main clientele is the type of customer who shops at thrift stores. The management thought it was really cool, not that we were doing pro bono, but that we'd done a Goodwill store. There was even an article about our pro bono work published in *Architectural Record* magazine.

From our perspective, the pro bono work and the community outreach we do allows us to think outside ourselves. If you are making money and business is good, this kind of project is right up there with continuing education and other kinds of employee development as a way to create a good sense of culture and training. But it's important to remember that the need is there—and sometimes greater—in slow economic times.

Hands On

Hands On Atlanta Headquarters
Location Atlanta, Georgia **Date** 2004 **Client** Hands On Atlanta **Client liaison** Tracy Hoover **Design firm** Jova/Daniels/Busby **Design team** Roy Abernathy, Rafael Diaz, Michael Rindsberg **Area** 53,000 sq. ft. **Cost** $650,000 **Estimated value of pro bono design services** $160,000 **Websites** www.handsonatlanta.org, www.jova.com

Tracy Hoover
Former CEO, Hands On Atlanta,
Atlanta, Georgia

Roy Abernathy
Principal, Jova/Daniels/
Busby,
Atlanta, Georgia

CLIENT

When this project began, Hands On Atlanta was being forced to move and didn't have much up-front cash. We were looking for a pretty unusual possibility—a landlord who would work with us on a ten-year lease with the possibility of lease-to-own. We didn't want a short-term lease because this was the fourth move in the life of the organization; we just couldn't continue to move every three to five years.

When we first saw the space that would become our home, we knew there was real potential. Jova/Daniels/Busby, because of its record and reputation of work with the nonprofit community in Atlanta, seemed like the perfect firm to help us. At the time, the space was raw. The architects helped us see past that and envision what it could be: cool, hip, and funky, but also very productive. Our organization connects thousands of Atlanta volunteers with more than 400 nonprofit service groups in the city. What drove the site selection and construction was a real desire for the building to become a volunteer headquarters.

In the lease, we negotiated funds to improve the space before we moved in. Jova/Daniels/Busby helped us maximize that very, very minimal per-square-foot amount and get a lot of materials donated. When we first moved into the building and walked funders through it, it was extremely powerful to be able to say, "Everything you see was donated." From cubicles to office furniture and even electronics, Jova/Daniels/Busby helped us find all the materials we needed from clients, partners, and vendors.

The firm's creative ways to save money also led to unique features. The light fixtures were on clearance at a local store, and one of the designers snatched all that were available to work them into the color scheme. The project had to incorporate in-kind and pro bono resources, as well as volunteers, as much as possible. Volunteers laid the carpet and put the cubicles together, and the firm coordinated all of that. The project involved some of our corporate partners, one of them being GE, which gave significant resources; the company is a major supporter of the organization and wanted to participate in the building in some way. ▷

ARCHITECT

The consulting company that I worked for before I joined Jova/Daniels/Busby had partnered with Hands On Atlanta a number of times, so you can imagine how I felt when I realized that my current firm was renovating a Jewish temple that was home to Hands On. You can also imagine how I felt when it became clear that this nonprofit that I cared about would be pushed out of that space. On the upside, Hands On realized that its space in the temple didn't really match up with its identity, what it was doing, or what it wanted to be. Jova/Daniels/Busby wanted to help ease this transition, so we offered to assist Hands On in finding a new home. ▷

Together we looked at a number of properties with the aim of positioning the nonprofit in a lease-to-own scenario, ideally in a building large enough that portions of it could be rented out to generate revenue. The building we decided on was an old fish-distribution facility. It had an original Georgian core with good bones; the quality was there, but too many layers had been added over time. There was one section where the previous tenants unloaded carts of fish and ice off of trains, the tracks for which still pass right behind the building. On the upper floor, there were very high ceilings and a lot of light, so we chose to make that the more public part of the building. ▸

We completed the project in four months because Hands On was getting pushed out of the temple. Our firm, along with Skanska, the contractor, donated its time, and we got IBM to donate lightly used carpeting from its own facilities. Hands On also had relationships with companies like Home Depot, Coca-Cola, the law firm Alston & Bird, and Accenture, where I worked previously. We developed a targeted shopping list of items we wanted from each company and asked for those materials, which was easier than saying, "We're doing a building. Do you have anything you could donate?" While material donations can be the answer to your prayers, without specific ▸

ideas, you can wind up with things you have no use for.

Hands On's staff, board, and volunteers took an active role in shaping the space. We had designed a wall with a patchwork of colors to highlight the diversity of the organization. The staff was painting it, and I got a call in the middle of a Saturday from volunteers who said, "You've got to come look at this; we think we have a problem." They had taped off and painted all the different shapes. The paint colors should have touched, but the tape they used created thick white lines between them. We ended up leaving the wall that way, because it looked quite good and became a focal point of the space.

The biggest success in my mind was finding a building that became a tool for Hands On. The space has really driven the organization and propelled it forward. The employees and volunteers have said it's the mirror image of the nonprofit. We've expanded Hands On twice now; they've taken over the whole building and purchased it as planned. Now that they have merged with the Points of Light Foundation, it is the preeminent organization for coordinating volunteerism in the country.

Jova/Daniels/Busby has always been very involved in the community, but I don't think the firm knew what to call its pro bono work before I came here. These kinds of projects have always been a pervasive part of the firm's practice. Often ▶

Having never been part of a process like this, I was delighted with the way the firm structured the design meetings. The designers took us through a process of roundtable conversations and stakeholder meetings that included our board, volunteers, and staff. That gave me a good sense of where the commonalities were and where we would need to make some compromises. They took on our big-picture vision—that the space should be open and collaborative, vibrant and welcoming—as well as action-oriented items, such as splitting up private and public areas. They asked us, "In your work spaces, how do you work together and which teams collaborate most?" They did a great job of balancing an aspirational vision of what the space should be with a practical, functional idea of what we needed.

Through the conversations with the firm, we came to think about our work spaces and our meeting spaces separately. The work space is designed with pods, cubicles, and a round table in the middle, so people can come together. Then we have a pool of conference spaces: some are small, some are large, some are private, some are more open. The smallest, which is called "the privacy room," is only a bit larger than a telephone booth. The largest can hold 100 people, which is approximately the number of volunteers we host at our weekly orientations. We can gather everyone together in this room, but when it is not in use, garage doors divide it into smaller spaces. Jova/Daniels/Busby did a fabulous job designing the building to flex up and down to accommodate our needs.

Our national organization, Hands On Network, has merged with another national organization, the Points of Light Foundation. Points of Light was located in Washington, D.C., at the time of the merger. I think many people assumed our headquarters would be located there, but thanks to this project, we had the more compelling space. For the Atlanta community, it was a real win for the national organization to be located here. The facility has become a gathering place. We offer our meeting spaces to any nonprofit or group of volunteers in Atlanta at no charge. One of our stakeholders calls it, "a campaign headquarters for the common good." It's a place where Atlanta comes together.

the younger members of our staff propose and lead pro bono projects, and they frequently end up on the boards for the organizations. As a firm, we see growth in communications, personal satisfaction, professional development, and networking, and our employees get a real handle on what kind of impact their skills can have in the community.

Kam Liu

Kam Liu Building
Location Chicago, Illinois **Date** 2004 **Client** Chinese American Service League **Client liaison**
Bernarda Wong **Design firm** Studio Gang Architects **Design team** Kara Boyd, Yuting Chen, Lynda Dossey,
William Emmick, Jeanne Gang, Kathleen O'Donnell, Mark Schendel, Juliane Wolf **Area** 36,000 sq. ft. **Cost**
$5.2 million **Estimated value of pro bono design services** $150,000 **Websites** www.caslservice.org,
www.studiogang.net

Kara Boyd
Project Architect,
Studio Gang Architects,
Chicago, Illinois

Bernarda Wong
Executive Director, Chinese American Service League,
Chicago, Illinois

ARCHITECT

The Kam Liu Building for CASL was one of Studio Gang's first projects. In the beginning, our rates were competitive, but the scope changed as the project went on and the complexities increased. We really wanted to keep the project going, and we wanted it to be done well. In the end, we donated resources to keep up the level of design and quality of the building. We donated a lot of our time and did the project at about 25 percent of cost, which paid for some of our expenses.

CASL is a community organization that started in a very grassroots way, which is something that stood out for me. When we started working with the group, there were ▶

CLIENT

In 2009, the Chinese American Service League (CASL) celebrated its thirtieth anniversary of providing new immigrants in the Midwest with employment assistance, language training, and other social services. Thirty years ago, I was the only staff member, and now we have a team of 300. In the early 1980s, we moved from a 700-square-foot apartment to a 10,000-square-foot building. Every year or two, we expanded.

When we brought on Studio Gang, we had five sites, one of which we owned and the rest we rented. The conditions in all of them were not the best. We had leaky skylights, so on rainy days, students and daycare kids had to be moved around to avoid the water. The sewage system also had problems. We decided it was time to take a leap of faith and try to raise money for a new building. The opportunity to build from scratch excited us, as did the opportunity to find an architect who understood our vision to provide services, atmosphere, and culture for our community. We ended up being able to acquire a piece of property, and we were on our way.

CASL had renovated a warehouse, but we had never constructed a brand new building, so we solicited bids from several architects. We narrowed it down to three firms and asked them to present to a committee that included several board members and me. We felt an energy with Studio Gang right away, and I also liked that we would be working with a woman-owned firm. Together we gathered a lot of informal feedback, talked to the community leaders, and had a number of sessions with elected community officials. Our program managers met with the architects regularly to go over classroom sizes, design, and the relationship between different programs. ▶

many different programs and fractured parts that made up the whole of the organization. CASL was going to be brought together in one place for the first time with this project. Studio Gang helped the organization envision and plan how its programs would function in one building.

CASL runs nearly fifteen different community programs. It is a lot to track and a lot of people to know and understand. We got to know how the individual programs and the organization as a whole worked, which was one of the keys to the project's success. It enabled our firm to design a building that functions very well for a complex and dense nonprofit. The new building presented a better face to the community, one that its members did not expect. A showcase building or a building that could make them proud was not a priority. It's not that CASL had low design standards; we simply exceeded its expectations.

The Chinese community played a role in the design process, particularly with contributions of materials. The building itself was actually pretty lean and efficient before we started, so there was not much to chop out, but there was pressure to downgrade materials. Jeanne Gang, the head of our firm, was very proactive and went out of her way to get more than the most basic materials donated. The titanium shingles are a result of her efforts and were donated by CASL's board chairman. ▸

CASL is such a powerful organization, but not in a top-down way. It impacts many people, and the community is so grateful to have the organization. Many people donated their time to us, meeting us and taking extra time to show us things. They introduced us to the Zhou Brothers, the Chicago-based artists who created the donor wall, a beautiful art piece in the lobby. The enthusiasm level of the community members was always very high and inspiring.

Our principals, Jeanne Gang and Mark Schendel, are great at turning something that at first seems like a disappointment into an asset. For example, there was not enough space for the second stairway we wanted to put in the building, so we had to add a fire escape. It quickly became a signature part of the building as well as a covered area for the playground and daycare play area.

A feng shui master consulted on the project and worked closely with us. We met often and took those considerations to heart. Architecturally, we initially wanted a space that you could see through from one side to another. We learned it would have allowed an unhealthy flow of chi in the building, so we changed the concept. By changing circulation for feng shui, we changed the way that people interact in the building in a really positive way.

Studio Gang has a good, ongoing relationship with CASL. I am there once every couple of months ▹

The titanium for the exterior of the building was donated by the chairman of our board of directors, Ernest Wong, who happens to have investments in that business. The material is wonderful, easy to clean, and shines and changes color in the sun at different times of the day. Studio Gang designed the titanium in diamond-shaped shingles that are like the scales of a dragon, the dragon being an ancient Chinese motif. In my mind, it also evokes the different waves of immigrants that come here; the immigrant populations are as different as the light that shines on the titanium and the colored shapes that are reflected. The Kam Liu Building is the only titanium building in the state of Illinois.

On the second floor is our big hall, which has a lot of glass. The architects wanted to make sure the sun would not beat down through the window, so they designed a lattice outside that looks like Chinese windows but also acts as a screen. The lattice is separated from the window, so one can walk outside on a little balcony. It is a really nice feature.

The grand hall bubbles with activity now that programming is all in a shared space. The hall is two stories with mirrors on one side and windows on the other. People mingle. Sometimes we have intergenerational events, like a ping-pong tournament in which the staff plays against the youth. In the past, everybody had to put on coats and go outside. Now we just walk down the stairs. People are closer together. Visitors also love the space, and we rent it out a lot.

The building is a wonderful improvement for my staff, and it makes our group much more efficient. Staff and clients do not have to wander from one building to another; they are directed to different floors. We also do not have to worry about fixing the roof and all those old problems. The headaches of the physical repairs are gone.

Through our new building, the community has been brought closer to us. More people come in because it is easier; it is a one-stop shop. A lot of other local organizations like our building. We end up hosting many meetings for the Chinese community, the larger Asian community, and sometimes beyond that. Those are real benefits.

The Chinese community is very proud of the finished product. People come and visit. The building is often mentioned in articles and at different meetings that we attend. Our funders are really impressed that we were able to pull together this campaign and create such a beautiful space. Everywhere we go, we hear funders tell each other to see the Kam Liu Building because it is such a wonderful place. We have won a lot of awards, and Mayor Daley was here recently and was amazed by the design.

to give a tour or some-
thing. It is great to see the
community thriving in
the space; users seem to
really love it. A big part
of the design was working
with them to figure out
how every given space can
accommodate two or
three different programs.
Studio Gang is proud
and happy that the orga-
nization is doing so well.
The project is also an
important element in our
portfolio. It has helped
us land other jobs by showing our ability to work
with meager means to
achieve good design.

Lavezzorio

Lavezzorio Community Center
Location Chicago, Illinois **Date** 2008 **Client** SOS Children's Villages Illinois **Client liaison** Tim McCormick
Design firm Studio Gang Architects **Design team** Yuting Chen, Lynda Dossey, Jeanne Gang, Jay Hoffman,
Thorsten Johann, Beth Kalin, Miriam Neet, Mauricio Sanchez, Mark Schendel, Schuyler Smith, Juliane Wolf,
Beth Zacherle **Area** 16,000 sq. ft. **Cost** $3.35 million **Estimated value of pro bono design services**
$320,000 **Websites** www.sosillinois.org, www.studiogang.net

Tim McCormick
CEO, SOS Children's Villages Illinois,
Chicago, Illinois

CLIENT

The SOS Children's Villages provide safe and supportive environments for foster children around the world. All children in the villages live with a trained foster parent, and many live with their biological siblings. Creating a center that is an asset for the whole neighborhood and that increases the programs we offer our foster families is a priority for all SOS projects. In our work in Africa and Asia, that might be a clinic or a school. The goal for the Lavezzorio Community Center in Chicago was to open a dialogue with the local community.

We are located in the Auburn Gresham neighborhood, which borders Inglewood and is one of the higher-crime areas in Chicago. Violence is just part of the landscape. At the same time, there's an awful lot of strong leadership stemming from the community. There are good people working very hard to keep their families thriving. When we began thinking about this center, we talked to community members and asked, "What does this neighborhood need most?" Their answer was quality, affordable daycare, so we designed the building around a daycare center. We also wanted a place that would be safe for the foster children to come to learn and develop. We wanted to strengthen families.

In selecting an architect, we looked at four criteria. First, we wanted someone who would be a partner, who would understand our mission and what we wanted to create. The second component was finding a firm that inspired us, and Jeanne Gang and her people did that and more. We weren't just looking for practicality and pragmatism; creativity was really important. The third criterion was an ability to work within our limited resources and help us solicit support and in-kind donations. The last component was for the firm to support and challenge us and make us a better organization. We got all four of those with Studio Gang. ▸

Jeanne Gang
Principal, Studio Gang
Architects,
Chicago, Illinois

ARCHITECT

We like to have at least one community building project going on in the office at any given time. So when we first interviewed with SOS Illinois, we knew from experience that this type of project ends up being pro bono to some degree; there's always donated time and effort. But the value is that you can have a big impact on a neighborhood, more of an impact than most paying jobs, which is exciting. Since the project went on for five years, we knew that we couldn't do everything pro bono, but it was about creating a balance. We have projects in the office that are more profitable, and those help even out what we spend on community projects.

SOS Illinois didn't have a very big budget, and they wanted us to incorporate a lot of in-kind materials and services. At first, it was a little frustrating because we would design a stairwell in concrete and then get steel donated. We eventually created a spreadsheet to manage donations that the owner and contractor thought they might get. In time, the materials became interchangeable, and we started thinking of the project more like a collage. It became critical to keep an open mind and be flexible about the design. ▸

Originally we secured a big donation of brick, so we planned the building around that. When the shipment fell through, we decided to leave the concrete exposed. Conceptually, we thought if we incorporated different concrete mixes from different contractors, it could be really interesting to play up the lines and layers. In the end, all the concrete was donated by one contractor, so we changed the mix slightly each time to bring a fluid quality to the wall. When you're doing a project that has these kinds of budget constraints, you definitely learn some tricks. This is what I love about architecture; every time you do a new project, you learn something new. ▷

The design process was educational. The leaders at Studio Gang came to SOS Illinois and met with parents and the kids. They immediately got their heads around why we exist and the type of work we needed done. They saw why this community center would be an anchor that supports our foster families in the village and the neighboring community. Studio Gang did their due diligence about SOS villages throughout the world, figuring out the mission we promote.

We were very fortunate as an organization to have an array of talented people in both development and construction. Our volunteer leadership participated in construction as well as the design process. Studio Gang helped us secure in-kind donations of everything from carpeting to bricks to faucets, and our general contractor, Bovis, was instrumental in working with the firm to incorporate those materials into construction. Bovis did the whole job pro bono.

Architects are innately well positioned to bring out the creativity in a project. Our architects from Studio Gang helped us understand how to be more creative with the resources we have; they taught us about flexibility and adaptability. The firm is a great and important partner for us, and it continues to be supportive of our mission.

The building's design reaffirms and strengthens our vision by providing transparency to the children. On a day-to-day basis, it costs us more money to keep the many windows clean, but the windows echo a value of allowing people to feel safe—people who have been in very vulnerable situations. We are working with kids who have been neglected, abused, and pushed to the periphery. Often this abuse happens in seclusion— behind closed doors, in basements, and so forth. The design gives ▸

children a sense of emotional and physical safety through the openness the building provides. The community center towers above all the other homes in a very purposeful manner so that someone is always looking over the children. It is the eye of the village.

When we look at the volume of people coming in and out every day, using our computers to find jobs and things like that, you can see that they feel safe here. In any given week, over 225 people access the community center. It is really an asset for the whole neighborhood.

Given what the foster kids go through, there is a great deal of sensitivity to how the staff members conduct their counseling sessions and meetings with the children's birth parents. We paid attention to having visibility between rooms so the kids felt safe. Also, the counseling rooms for the foster kids are on the second floor for greater security.

Our idea was to have a gathering space for both kids from the foster families and the neighborhood kids, since this building really bridges the two. There are spaces that can be used for just about anything. And then there is the daycare, which is mainly for the community children. We kept the space open and built kid-friendly design ▸

features, like the staircase, to encourage activity and playfulness. For the foster kids, a lot of their lives have been pretty traumatic; we wanted to make the place fun and uplifting. Creating a building that has a strong identity was also important. It is a space that the community can be proud of. People have accepted it and respected it; there's no graffiti or vandalism.

In pro bono work, you need to have patience. Usually architects do these projects when they are just starting out, and they really want it to be good, but it takes a long time. You have to go with the flow and not get freaked out when the project gets put on hold so the organization can try to raise money.

Pro bono work is part of our office ethos. It feels good to serve people, and it lets us get to know a different side of Chicago. Sometimes you end up working a lot at your office and staying in your own little area, so when you do a community project, you really discover that neighborhood. Learning to do things in a less expensive way also creates a nice design effect. It can be heartbreaking sometimes when things don't work out, but everything you do expands your toolkit.

Yawkey

Yawkey Distribution Center
Location Boston, Massachusetts **Date** 2009 **Client** Greater Boston Food Bank **Client liaison** Carol Tienken **Design firm** Chan Krieger NBBJ **Design team** Brad Cooper, Michael Dembowski, Courtney Erwin, Michael Fields, Stephen Gray, Andrew Hartness, Jennifer Lee, Florin Luca, Adrienne Mossler, Andrew Richard, Tom Sieniewicz, Gary Wang, Jennifer Wong, Piper Woodworth **Area** 117,000 sq. ft. **Cost** $25 million **Estimated value of pro bono design services** $300,000 **Websites** www.gbfb.org, www.chankrieger.com

Tom Sieniewicz
Principal, Chan Krieger
NBBJ,
Boston, Massachusetts

ARCHITECT

During this project for the Greater Boston Food Bank, I became a food banker; I became an advocate for issues relating to hunger. A food bank, by its very nature, is a sustainable approach to social justice. If you want to be part of the most detailed and effective solution, you wear your client's uniform and own the organization's issue, because you're building a machine that is going to help the staff serve people on a massive scale.

At the very start of our work together, before we had even put pen to paper, the food bank's leaders asked to hear my vision of the building. I responded by saying that my vision was for people in Boston to drive by and look up at a wall that had the warmth of the hearth of a fireplace, and that prominent wall and the building itself would look substantial, like the work of the food bank.

It's hard to find a spokesperson for the issue of hunger, particularly among people who utilize a food bank. There's always some amount of ▸

Carol Tienken
COO, Greater Boston Food Bank,
Boston, Massachusetts

CLIENT

While the Greater Boston Food Bank's Yawkey Distribution Center functions primarily as a warehouse, its visibility as a landmark along a major freeway coming into Boston made the center's design critical to its success. We wanted to have something more than just a square building or a structure that looked like it belonged in an industrial park and didn't have a lot of character. The unusual shape of the lot and our desire to have a green, sustainable building meant that bringing on an architect was our best solution. Tom Sieniewicz stood out in our search. His love of architecture and his understanding of what we needed were immediately clear.

We wanted to ensure that there was as much synergy as possible between the architect and the construction company, so we also selected Tom's firm because of its demonstrated ability to collaborate with a contractor. During the entire construction process, even when we were value-engineering, Chan Krieger NBBJ maintained an amazing degree of engagement and support.

We were blown away by the firm's commitment to, and involvement with, the building. The team members immersed themselves in food banking and learning how our particular supply chain works. The architects, at their own expense, went with me to see other food banks in several cities to explore the positives and negatives of those designs. We wanted to see how we might incorporate features that worked there into our own space and also see what we didn't want to do. This helped us identify the operational layout of the new distribution center. And, as they say, form followed function. ▸

In essence, Tom and his team became part of our staff and got to know everyone. They were accessible and very patient in explaining the nuances of each step in the design process. We met with the architects routinely during that time, and we included the construction company, too.

The new building has increased our capacity by a factor of four. It has provided us with a bright, large, clean, inviting space in which to work and serve our customers. So much thought went into the design, including little things that most of the staff didn't expect. The light in the building is amazing. There are areas for private telephone calls, and there is filtered water for all of the large sinks. The HVAC system keeps even the non-air-conditioned spaces relatively cool. The orientation of the building, relative to the street, works for truck drivers, which is important for managing traffic in the neighborhood.

The interest in the new building has been phenomenal. People often think of a food bank as a pantry in the basement of a church. But we're one of the largest food banks in the country—we distribute millions of pounds of food products annually to a huge network of other agencies in the state, like soup kitchens, homeless shelters, and senior centers. Now that the building is completed, I think the public is getting a better sense of what we are. Visitors, agencies, and staff all have made positive comments. We had a major fund-raising event two weeks after the move, and we were oversubscribed for attendance. The building even has "Greater Boston Food Bank" silhouetted against the sky as you come into the city. We are very pleased with that because it makes people aware of our presence.

We couldn't have asked for anything more at the beginning, middle, or end of our building project. Both Chan Krieger NBBJ and Consigli Construction, our contractor, are right here beside us as we continue to resolve issues with the building. I wish that everyone getting involved in something of this scope and magnitude could have the opportunity to work with the caliber of team that we had. Their creativity and commitment were unparalleled and unwavering. The fact that the architects had a wonderful sense of humor didn't hurt either. I hope they are as proud of the project as we are.

humiliation when people can no longer provide for themselves. So we volunteered our time to explain and promote the project and raise money and excitement for the building in the wider community. The food bank staff actually took me aside and said, "We love it when you talk about 'us' and blur the relationship between your firm and the food bank. We're on the same team, and we're wearing the same jersey—we love that."

Our buildings have an industrial look, and this is clearly an industrial building at heart. We knew we could take that vernacular and make something that was pretty formally interesting. I traveled to Atlanta and Chicago on my own time to observe a number of food banks, and I sent some of my staff, at our expense, to visit another major facility in Cleveland, which is a pretty remarkable place.

We also went to Vermont to see a particular refrigeration device they use at a food bank there. We ended up adapting that system to this project, but it had never been done on this scale before. It's a very simple idea: On many days of the year, the outside air in Boston is well below the temperature you need for food refrigeration. If you're maintaining large volumes of cool air, you bottle that outside air and drive it into the freezers and coolers. Then you don't have to run the refrigeration systems when the outside air temperature is below what it has to be inside. ▸

We are very aware that there is a code of ethics that governs our profession; people need to make their livings from what we do, and so we are very careful about whom we give our services to and under what circumstances. At the beginning of the process, I went to my partners and told them the food bank was looking for some help. The partners came up with the idea that we would donate all the principals' time; over the course of the project, it was somewhere in excess of $300,000.

Beyond that, I went to each of the consultants on our team and asked what he or she could do on behalf of the nonprofit. To a tee, every person reduced his or her fees to some degree in recognition of the mission of the food bank. So it wasn't just us. Hunger is such an understandable human condition that when I turned to a consultant or vendor and said, "It's about feeding hungry people," nobody ever said, "No." No one ever turned me down; nobody ever said they wouldn't do it. It gives you great power to just ask.

People don't work in this firm unless they share our values about giving back. A lot of young people want to work here just because of our reputation for being civic minded. The value to the firm in giving back is that it is very good for morale. The Yawkey Distribution Center project has been a great, positive thing that attracts high-quality, thoughtful, compassionate, hard-working, serious young designers and architects.

Education

Bridge School

The Bridge School
Location Hillsborough, California **Date** 2007 **Client** The Bridge School **Client liaison** Vicki Casella **Design firm** WRNS Studio **Design team** Sam Nunes, David Shiwotsuka, Pauline Souza, Melinda Turner, Adam Woltag **Area** 1,210 sq. ft. **Cost** $550,000 **Estimated value of pro bono design services** $250,000 **Websites** www.bridgeschool.org, www.wrnsstudio.com

Vicki Casella
Executive Director, The Bridge School,
Hillsborough, California

CLIENT

The Bridge School is a nonprofit school for children with severe physical impairments and complex communication needs. Our children generally require assistance to walk, and speech is not their primary mode of communication. Kids come here, and we work intensively with them to develop an effective communication system, which sometimes means beginning the reading and writing process from scratch. Once they have an effective way to communicate with others, they leave the Bridge School and go back to their own schools.

Since our founding in 1986, two of our students have gone on to graduate from college, one from San Francisco State University and one from the University of California, Berkeley, and we have another former student who currently is a junior at Berkeley. These children were underserved in their public school placements, but after working with our staff, they returned to their high schools and graduated.

We have a strong research program to gather and analyze evidence from our practices, and it used to be housed in a separate facility from the school. This created the mentality that it was a separate program, and that was not my vision of the research component of our work. When I took over as director, I wanted to bring the education and research programs together on the same campus.

There were other problems with our existing building. I wanted to expand to have more instructional space, because our children need an environment that is accessible and geared toward their developmental levels. With more space, we could have more appropriate groupings of students and more room for technology. We also needed a protected outside area, so our kids could go out and get fresh air even on bad weather days.

To address our challenges, we enlisted the architects at WRNS Studio. Everyone at the school was involved in talking to them, but our teaching staff had lots of input since they know exactly what they need in the classroom. The team from WRNS also came down to the school to meet the children and see how they move around. The architects came up with some really simple solutions—things that may not sound fancy but that accomplish all of our goals. ▷

Pauline Souza
Associate Principal,
WRNS Studio,
San Francisco, California

ARCHITECT

The Bridge School is housed in a series of very modest trailers that sit on property belonging to a public school that's part of the Hillsborough City School District, one of our firm's clients. Vicki Casella, who directs the Bridge School, wanted to create a warm and supportive setting with simple components, and she was looking for a true partner, a firm that would do more than simply put plans together and secure permits. We had been interested in the Bridge School's approach to integrating kids with certain disabilities into the conventional school system, so we took on the project pro bono.

Vicki was great at explaining what the school needed, but she also introduced us to the teachers ▷

and children so we could directly hear and see their needs. They needed more classroom space, and they needed more room for families to come in and observe their kids and for teachers to have some quiet areas for themselves. We were working with very little money and very little square footage, but we wanted to turn their existing trailers into more than just trailers. We did the usual functional programming—figuring out layouts and where best to place outlets and doors—but more important, we worked on a solution to one main necessity that we identified from our time with the students: The kids needed to participate with each other. The idea of creating a connecting deck, an outdoor classroom, came from that understanding. It makes the space an area where the kids can truly be outside instead of it simply being the space between two trailers.

Designing schools, as we often do, we are used to very modest materials, but we also had to shed any preconceptions of what a trailer or a modular building is. We talked to the trailer manufacturers to try to push them to think differently, to really engage in the manufacturing process and not just assemble the components and fix them to the deck. It might be funny for folks to hear that we did three-dimensional modeling and tested materials just to assemble some trailers and a deck, but we tried hard to think about every aspect of the teaching environments and indoor/outdoor space. We tackled it with all the energy we ▶

would use on one of our fee-generating projects.

The final design developed from the usual balance of cost, schedule, and program. We placed a canopy over the deck to protect the kids from sun and rain. We fit in a space at the end of the sequence of trailers that connected to what we call "the jungle" at the public school. It is a grove of eucalyptus trees and playground structures where all the kids go to play. By connecting the jungle, a place with a lot of significance for students from both schools, to the Bridge School's outdoor space, we really bridged the gap between the two student bodies.

This project took place very early in WRNS's lifetime as a firm. We were literally just unpacking the boxes in our office, and we had fewer jobs, so we were able to give the Bridge School a good amount of attention. It also was an opportunity to give our younger staff more experience. We had a fairly young architect on board, and because this was the right size and the right client, it gave her an opportunity to go deeper into a project. Those of us who were more senior had done some pro bono work with our previous firms, but we were operating as individuals, not as a business. When our firm was getting started, it was a good time to take on a small project like this.

All of the engineering and some of the contracting were also done pro bono. I didn't even have to give the hard sell to those ▶

Our new space is a truly instructional environment, and we use it to maximize the potential of these children. Before, it took lots of time to break down a space or transition from one activity to another, which was problematic because we have several students who are highly distractible. With the new renovations, we are able to separate parts of the room, and the children can get to work with minimal disruption. We also can put up black partitions that contrast with whatever object we are holding in front of the students. It's a small thing, but visual processing is key for our children, and those are the details they needed.

The kids love the new space! Their favorite part is the deck. WRNS designed a beautiful deck with a canopy over it, and it has become a heavily used outdoor area for our students and staff. They can go out there and just be outside, and it also gives the kids direct access to a beautiful garden that the parents planted. The deck meets our aesthetic sensibility and has exceeded our expectations in terms of its use and functionality. Having a nice facility allows us to show others what we're doing, and it makes us take even greater pride in our work. Neil Young is one of our founding board members, and he is very particular about how things look and work. We didn't want to look like we're a special education school, and WRNS took on that challenge.

The architects were able to grasp the whole concept, vision, and mission of our school without difficulty. They signed on immediately and brought great ideas. Not only did they provide all the services that the firm offers, but Pauline Souza, in particular, was also phenomenal in getting everyone else involved—engineers, surveyors, and contractors—to donate their services. Only because of WRNS's involvement were we able to afford this expansion.

The team at WRNS didn't see our children's limitations; they saw their potential. I think that was part of their dedication—to ensure we had a facility that would help achieve our goal of maximizing the potential of these children. It is a rare insight, and more than anything, we are grateful for that sense of humanity.

contributors; I just presented it as an opportunity, and everyone said, "Absolutely, I want in." We even talked as a group about making the building as sustainable as possible. Each of those firms had a different reason for wanting to participate. Either people had members of their families with similar disabilities, or they had a history of teaching, or that spirit was just a part of who they are. I was surprised, on such a small project, to find so many people who wanted to help.

I think the project pushed some of our senior designers to think differently, too. We didn't expect that it could be done so simply. It's important to give credit to structures that aren't necessarily made of the most exotic materials or created with the most state-of-the-art assembly techniques. This has been such a worthy job that I think we all feel changed by it.

Calvin Hill

Elizabeth Gray and
Alan Organschi
Principals, Gray Organschi
Architecture,
New Haven, Connecticut

Calvin Hill School Day Care Center Art Studios
Location New Haven, Connecticut **Date** 2004 **Client** Calvin Hill School Day Care Center and Kitty Lustman-Findling Kindergarten **Client liaison** Carla Horwitz **Design firm** Gray Organschi Architecture **Design team** Kyle Bradley, Elizabeth Gray, Alan Organschi **Area** 1,100 sq. ft. **Cost** $350,000 **Estimated value of pro bono design services** $99,000 **Websites** www.calvinhilldaycare.org, www.grayorganschi.com

Carla Horwitz
Director, Calvin Hill School Day Care Center
and Kitty Lustman-Findling Kindergarten,
New Haven, Connecticut

CLIENT

The Calvin Hill School Day Care Center and Kitty Lustman-Findling Kindergarten was started by Yale University undergraduates in 1971 to provide high-quality, early-childhood education to children from families that might not be able to otherwise afford it. This remains the mission today. Our educational model is based on helping children make sense of the many new symbols in their worlds and use their own visual thinking, creativity, and expression in learning.

There is a long history of children of architects attending Calvin Hill, as well as a history of parental involvement at the school. In the past, parents have done a great deal of fund-raising and have undertaken several renovation projects, including the addition of the kindergarten in 1983. Parents here get bitten by the Calvin Hill bug. When Lisa Gray and Alan Organschi enrolled their son in the kindergarten, they got very excited about the school, and then they invited the class to their studio. They got involved almost immediately.

Lisa and Alan were very intrigued by, and enthusiastic about, my idea of creating spaces for art, music, and movement on the first and second levels of the building. They really understood the way we work. All of our spaces are designed with aesthetics in mind, but beauty, nature, light, and transparency are the keystones of this project. The addition that Lisa and Alan built absolutely embraces, enhances, and supports each of those elements.

Lisa, Alan, and I had several conversations about what I envisioned for the project, and then we had to sell it to my board. Being a small non-profit, we also had budget constraints to keep in mind, even though there was pro bono work involved. We formed a building committee and had ▸

ARCHITECT

We are partners in life as well as in our work. We have two kids, and our younger child went to the Calvin Hill School for a year. His experience there was so creative and flexible. The program was geared toward generating curiosity; we were really impressed with it. During our year there, the school's staff and board spoke of their interest in creating an arts space that would allow children to do sustained projects.

We were so convinced of the worth of this program for our own child and other kids that we decided to jump in and help make it happen. Even before we signed on, the school staff was showing us images of schools in Italy that they wanted to mirror, just because they knew that we were architects. They were passionate, and it was clear that they were aware of how good design can positively impact learning. We knew they would be fantastic collaborators; however, it was also clear that this was not going to happen unless we offered some of our services pro bono.

For us, Calvin Hill was the perfect pro bono project. In a pro bono arrangement, you want to be as efficient as possible. Having an extremely knowledgeable director at the school made the process very straightforward because the board gave her latitude and trusted her. She visited other schools that she thought worked well, and ▸

150
Calvin Hill
Day Care Center

Kitty Lustman-Findling
Kindergarten

they tended to be modern, open spaces, which was in line with the kind of work that we do. It was a good match. The time frame was really tight, but even that helped keep the project on track.

In our discussions with the director, a few things became clear. The school wanted its program to encourage kids to establish a direct relationship with the outdoors. The art rooms on both floors of the new structure are designed to have an indoor/outdoor feel. For us, it was important to separate the old spaces from the new spaces through the choice of materials. We also did some neat stuff in the addition, such as using clear pipes in the sinks so the kids can see paint go down the drain and start to understand where the water goes.

The design was greatly influenced by the site, which has a view of New Haven to the east. We also wanted to take advantage of an underused part of the site, the adjoining side alley. The teachers were happy to try to make something of it, so we got permission to consolidate a fire lane that Yale owned to make a wider lot for a playground and added a new entry for the school. Previously everyone entered through a garage door on the front of the building. Now the new second-floor overhang provides a protected entry, which is nice in the rain.

We also did construction management for the project free of charge, so we organized all of the subcontractors and bought the materials at cost. We effectively took ▸

The Power of Pro Bono

on the question of how to get the project done for the school. In certain cases, we had to find donated materials, but even with the small budget, we wanted to include some high-quality materials for the kids to interact with. Working pro bono allowed us to keep some elements in the project that we otherwise couldn't have afforded. We have a full workshop in our office and Alan has a background in construction, so we were able to deliver certain built elements at very low costs.

In terms of long-term benefits, there was a very good feeling in our office while Calvin Hill was going up. Everybody knew that it was the focus of the office and different staff members were constantly going over to work on the project. You can't overstate what a good thing it was for the office to be physically involved like that. Through this project, we gained exposure to early-childhood work. We believe that kids learn better in spaces that are thoughtfully designed. Too often you see daycare centers stuck in old strip malls. We are now very committed to designing engaging early-childhood facilities, and that really began with this job.

two years' worth of meetings. We discussed preliminary sketches from Alan and Lisa, and they refined those and presented them to us. They were extremely receptive to feedback.

Once the design was finalized, we had a very narrow window for the project to get done. The firm had to do a lot of the site work and lay the slabs while the school was on break for a week in March. We were also trying to raise $350,000 at the same time. This total did not include the construction management, so Lisa and Alan donated those services as well. It was a gift of unbelievable proportions. Kyle Bradley, from Alan and Lisa's office, was here every day and managed everything wonderfully. He actually negotiated all of the permits with Yale and came through with everything that was required. I also still always had access to Lisa and Alan.

The children got to see the building go up from start to finish. We incorporated lessons on how buildings are made into the curriculum through block building and in the sandbox. The crew members were great and were very sweet to the children. Just by having the workers around, the kids got to see something important happening and the way that people work with large materials. Having this happening on-site enhanced the learning experience. The kids would draw what they saw and write stories about the new space. Then they would give the stories to the subcontractors.

The new spaces are extremely beautiful, and they bring the outside in. They enable a whole other part of the curriculum to be developed not only for art but for music as well. They have also provided additional benefits that we did not expect, such as using the space for an undergraduate course that I teach for the Yale Child Study Center. I can also have board meetings for the school here, and adults can sit and talk to each other on real chairs.

Most important, the teachers are able to do a whole lot more with the kids thanks to this space. We can leave projects up and create large murals. We can set up a water table and have the children work on it in the morning and then come back to it. You can't do that in a regular classroom, because you have to clean up all the time. It is just a much better process for children to develop their potential and also for teachers to think about the development of children's minds.

Hanna Fenichel

Hanna Fenichel Center for Child Development
Location Solana Beach, California **Date** 2007 **Client** Hanna Fenichel Center for Child Development **Client liaison** Sarah Hillier **Design firm** Stephen Dalton Architects **Design team** Stephen Dalton, Cassandra Inman, Teri Wilson **Area** 2,350 sq. ft. **Cost** $300,000 **Estimated value of pro bono design services** $16,300 **Websites** www.hannafenichel.com, www.sdarchitects.net

Sarah Hillier
Director, Hanna Fenichel Center for Child Development,
Solana Beach, California

CLIENT

Before we acquired our current property in 2001, the previous owners had given the building numerous additions and renovations, but nothing was done in a consistent or thoughtful manner. Initially we simply wanted to complete some safety upgrades to the school's entry; however, we soon decided to give the entire building a facelift. Once we realized the scale of the project, we sought the services of an architect and the input of our active parent community. Thanks to a suggestion from the parent of a former student, we met with and chose Stephen Dalton Architects. Steve was professional, friendly, and really listened to our needs and concerns. His style worked with what we had on the exterior. He understood our mission, and he possessed a playful, joyful quality that really fit with who we are.

Our communication with Steve proved to be quite easy. The school's site committee, made up of current and former parents, was admittedly a tough group to work with but only because it had the children's best interests at heart. Members attended every meeting and scrutinized every design for safety. They asked, "How many children per square foot can be in a classroom? How many bathrooms, sinks, and toilets are required?" Steve, being a parent himself, understood where they were coming from. He was very understanding and receptive.

It took four years of serious fund-raising to accomplish our goal, and we started interviewing architects a year in advance of physically beginning the work. Construction began in the summer of 2007, and the school was closed for ten weeks. We were amazed that the whole process could happen so fast. We aimed to start school the day after Labor Day and only had to put that off by a week.

The process of agreeing on a design involved extensive discussions. Solana Beach is an interesting community, especially where our school is located. Nothing really ties the area together except for the beach. As a result, our thinking was to have a beach cottage motif in the design. Steve did his best, but we found that unless there was a thorough overhaul of the building, this would not be possible. We also had a budget to keep in mind. Steve was very diplomatic in working with us and understood that everyone wanted to have his or her say. The design that we ended up choosing was controversial at the start, because it was not ▶

Stephen Dalton
Principal, Stephen Dalton Architects,
Solana Beach, California

ARCHITECT

My firm was just over a year old when we became involved in the Hanna Fenichel Center for Child Development. Before starting my own firm, I had worked mainly on high-budget projects, such as large mansions in gated communities. I felt like my efforts benefited a very small group of people, so part of my goal when I established my firm was to become more involved in the community—to take on projects that affect more people and have more visibility.

We toured the facility with the center's director, Sarah Hillier, before we started the design. We met the teachers, saw their process, and gained a sense of how the school operates. That helped us hone in on the functional requirements. We worked in collaboration with the school's site committee, a team comprised of ▶

Sarah and several parents. At that time, they didn't really know what their budget would be in the end. As part of my pro bono service, I produced renderings that they could show their board of directors and parents to aid fund-raising efforts. Once the design became more clearly defined, it was easier to raise money for the project.

There proved to be much discussion surrounding the design process. Our strategy was not to dig in our heels, but to remain open to other options. For a few months, we had worked with a certain group of parents, and then new faces started showing up at the meetings. Those people wanted to take the design in a different direction. In the end, we worked with the people who had shown the most interest early on, who we felt were the key members of the committee, and helped them become advocates for the design. Ultimately they convinced the others that the design we had developed was the right one for the project.

It was a very straightforward scheme. Because of the budget, we limited ourselves to color and pattern modifications—two things that couldn't be value-engineered out of the project. We kept the forms very simple and used clean, modern lines, relying on bright colors, intricate patterns and textures to create visual interest for the front entrance. The metallic panels on the front were initially going to be a bluish green stainless steel, but they were changed ▸

to Trespa, which is a
cheaper laminate. The
panels have a metallic
sheen, so varying the
color pattern got us the
texture we wanted.

Not relying on expensive
materials for visual impact
was a success throughout.
Things as cheap as a gal-
lon of paint maintained
the design but kept project
costs low. We didn't over-
reach, which would have
forced us to later com-
promise our intentions.
Even though the services
were pro bono, the client
was really interested in
good design and doing the
right thing. I still receive
feedback from the center
expressing how happy ev-
eryone is with the improvements to the facility, and
we continue to get calls to
consult on smaller projects
around the school. ▸

what we originally envisioned. But we came to realize that it did, in fact, best support the integrity of the site and the building. Steve's ultimate design is beautiful, and we all love it.

The changes have provided a welcoming and inviting place for the children, staff, and families. Steve created a safer and more attractive entrance, which was our top goal. We also have a wider overhang covering a walkway leading into our classrooms, which protects us from the elements. Moreover, he helped the building become more efficient by establishing much-needed larger spaces in a creative way. We now have a big ADA-accessible adult restroom. In addition, our kitchen space is much more spacious. We jokingly refer to it as our "great room."

The building evokes a sense of wonder, and encourages students to explore, discover, and learn. Steve utilized materials and a color scheme—bright orange, red, and yellow—that make it very playful. That is what we wanted, and it was really what sold us on the design.

The renovation has given the Hanna Fenichel Center for Child Development more recognition in the community, and in many ways, it has enhanced the overall feeling in the neighborhood. We meld with the community, but we also stand out more as a school. The center continues to be recognized by professional organizations in both the architecture and education worlds.

In the end, when a colleague and I totaled our hours, we found we had donated about 2 percent of our annual billable hours toward this job. The Hanna Fenichel Center was a great start to my pro bono work. One of the most important benefits has been using the project to market my firm, grow our portfolio, and expand our project types. We received a design award for this project from the American Institute of Architects in 2009, which has spurred us to publish and publicize our work. The other thing is the "feel good" aspect. We did something good for the children and the community as a whole.

KIPP

KIPP Academy Campus
Location Houston, Texas **Date** 2007 **Client** KIPP: Houston **Client liaison** Katy Hays **Design firm** Gensler
Design team Rob Bradford, Barry Moore, Dean Strombom, Lester Yuen **Area** 36 acres **Cost** $20.8 million
Estimated value of pro bono design services $312,000 **Websites** www.kipphouston.org,
www.gensler.com

Katy Hays
Assistant Superintendent, Institutional Advancement, KIPP: Houston,
Houston, Texas

CLIENT We collaborated with Gensler on the design of our flagship campus because we saw a strong match with the firm in terms of our missions and values. The principal architects seemed to particularly understand the culture we were trying to create and our need to be cost-efficient.

In working with Gensler's team, we saw that they fit our motto: "Work hard, be nice." The team accommodated our organization and dealt with a group of people who, at the time, was relatively young and inexperienced. The Knowledge Is Power Program (KIPP) was founded fifteen years ago by two young men who had been core members of Teach for America. They were two years out of college when they developed KIPP, and now there are eighty-three schools across the country. KIPP is a movement, not just a small group of schools.

Gensler was working with people who believe anything is possible, even if it seems difficult to pull off. Instead of stifling our vision, they were great listeners who became personal supporters of the school. The architectural team really went the extra mile to ensure that the buildings opened on time, particularly because it is impossible to start the school year late.

Rob Bradford and
Dean Strombom
Associate and Principal,
Gensler,
Houston, Texas

ARCHITECT Everyone in Gensler's Houston office who worked on this project has a personal story about why he or she is passionate about KIPP. Typically architecture serves wealthy clients, and we always love to see what it can do for those who do not normally benefit from design.

At the outset, Mike Feinberg, cofounder of KIPP, stressed his philosophy that "we can teach kids anywhere." Mike also expressed that he is not in the business of building temples, meaning he did not want the new campus to be too flashy. We had to work hard to get him to understand the value of design and what it could contribute to his program. Today he understands ▸

The main difference at the flagship campus now is that we actually have classrooms, whereas before we taught in temporary spaces. Since we are an open-enrollment charter school, classes are big, with twenty-eight to thirty students. Each classroom has a ton of whiteboards to help kids be organized and disciplined; our temporary buildings did not have space for such amenities. The rooms are really blank slates so that each class can be shaped based on the identity of the teacher and students. Instead of having a central campus library, many classrooms have their own individual libraries crafted by each teacher. Teachers also select the furniture and can have traditional desks, tables, and chairs, and sometimes even couches. Each room is flexible and reflects the personality and purpose of the teacher.

KIPP focuses on educating low-income and underserved kids. We want our kids to have opportunities and experiences that mirror those provided at the best college-prep schools, which, in most cases, have outstanding facilities. When you come from a place that is not really great, it shapes your frame of reference. We do not want our kids to feel foreign when moving to nicer environments for college. Gensler's design makes the kids feel like they come from someplace special. ▸

154   **The Power of Pro Bono**

Building the flagship campus has also greatly helped KIPP with fundraising. The campus is like an anchor; it gives us credibility and lets the community know that we are here to stay. We purposely did not build a fence around the school because we did not want to set ourselves apart from the community. We want our campuses to become the centers of their communities, as the Houston campus has. Our students have long days there. Classes run from 7:30 a.m. to 5:30 p.m., and with kids participating in after-school sports and activities, the facility is usually active until 9:00 p.m. We also offer adult classes in the evening to teach the parents computer and financial literacy.

Our program, including the completion of the flagship campus, is working to rebrand the image of education. KIPP: Houston has a waiting list of about 4,500 kids, most of them wanting to come here. In our old temporary spaces, we used to have to work to get kids to come to the school, but when parents see the flagship campus, they want their kids to be a part of it.

If we could afford it, we would build these campuses all over the country. It was nice to be in control of our own destiny and start from scratch, rather than renovating an old building. We are also in it for the long haul with Gensler. We may know what we want, but Gensler truly helps us get there.

and believes in it, but throughout the process, Mike was always challenging our design team to demonstrate the value that the kids would get from each new proposal or suggestion. We focused heavily on the natural lighting and spatial volume in the buildings as two key elements that could create better learning environments. These are things that we did not have to spend a lot of money on, but they created a high impact in terms of learning.

The new campus really expresses KIPP's values and work. Our design team spent a lot of time observing the children throughout the day so we could create a dynamic learning environment. For example, in the KIPP high school, we grouped the main reception area and the learning center together into a two-story space. The classroom wings emerge from this central zone. Designing the active spaces of the program together creates an engaging area for the students to meet in formal and informal arrangements without disturbing the classrooms.

The courtyard, which connects the elementary school, middle school, and gym, is another favorite area on the campus. Once the campus was completed, it really came to life. We planted a red oak tree in its center and designed a tricycle track that encircles the space. The high school just held its first commencement ceremony there. It is a unifying element of the campus and is used both actively and as a quiet study area. ▶

Gensler's graphic-design team focused on designing the symbols and slogans present throughout the KIPP school. When we entered the campus, we were literally bowled over by the slogans on the walls, and we were impressed by their inspirational quality. Our team converted the slogans into murals and wayfinding devices throughout the campus. These little things help knit the collection of buildings together into a cohesive whole.

In terms of the buildings' overall aesthetic, we focused on creating a utilitarian look that is interrupted by moments of color. Since it's inexpensive, we used paint to incorporate primary colors—yellow, red, and blue—in the space, giving the school a punch within a neutral palette of corrugated metal. KIPP felt the colors connected with its creativity. In fact, we had to guide the team away from using too much color, which would reduce the impact.

The shapes of the windows are also unique. We developed the scheme when Elliot Whitney, the school leader at KIPP Academy Middle School, told us that the school's philosophy embraces the idea of "ordered chaos." We then used the windows to create distinct cutouts on the long, corrugated-metal facades. If you step back, you can see the pattern and organization in the seemingly disordered wall. Furthermore, the shapes help break up the long facade that faces a public street and would otherwise be mundane. ▸

Gensler has benefited from our involvement with KIPP, as the project has brought in referrals and more business. Corporate clients who donate to KIPP have recognized what Gensler has done for the organization. They see the benefit from a design perspective and want it for their own businesses. We have also been contacted by other public and charter schools that want to see what design can do for their facilities.

Our relationship with KIPP has evolved, and we are now designing more schools for the organization. When we started, we were just the architects, but throughout the process they had to "KIPP-nitize" us. Now they consider us part of their family.

L!brary Initiative

Robin Hood L!brary Initiative
Location New York, New York **Date** 2001–9 **Client** Robin Hood Foundation **Design team** 17 architecture firms; Pentagram, graphic design **Estimated value of pro bono design services** Not available **Websites** www.robinhood.org, www.pentagram.com

1100 Architect

P.S. 46, Edward C. Blum, Brooklyn
P.S. 147, Isaac Remsen, Brooklyn
P.S. 274, Kosciusko, Brooklyn
P.S. 81, Jean Paul Richter, Queens
P.S. 105, The Bay School, Queens
P.S. 201, Kissena, Queens
P.S. 16, John J. Driscoll School, Staten Island

Alexander Gorlin Architect

C.S. 92, Bronx

Dean Wolf Architects

P.S. 151, Mary D. Carter, Queens

Deborah Berke Architect

P.S. 46, Arthur Tappan, Manhattan

Della Valle Bernheimer

P.S. 18, John Greenleaf Whitter School, Staten Island

Gluckman Mayner Architects

P.S. 48, Joseph R. Drake, Bronx
P.S. 64, Pura Belpre, Bronx
P.S. 154, John D. Hyatt, Bronx
P.S. 146, Anna M. Short, Manhattan
P.S. 189, Manhattan
P.S. 192, Jacob H. Schiff, Manhattan

Helfand Myerberg Guggenheimer Architects

P.S. 50, Clara Barton, Bronx

HMA2 Architects

P.S. 135, Sheldon A. Brookner, Brooklyn
P.S. 164, Caesar Rodney, Brooklyn

P.S. 216, Arturo Toscanini, Brooklyn
P.S. 323, Brooklyn
P.S. 335, Granville Woods, Brooklyn

Leroy Street Studio

P.S. 110, Florence Nightingale School, Manhattan
P.S. 31, William T. Davis, Staten Island

Paul Bennett Architect

P.S. 165, Ida Posner, Brooklyn

Richard H. Lewis Architect

P.S. 36, Union Port, Bronx
P.S. 47, John Randolph, Bronx
P.S. 69, The New Vision School, Bronx
P.S. 93, Albert G. Oliver, Bronx
P.S. 96, Richard Rodgers, Bronx
P.S. 186, Walter J. Damrosch, Bronx
P.S. 196, Bronx
P.S. 10, Magnet School of Math, Science, and Design, Brooklyn
P.S. 184, Newport, Brooklyn
P.S. 287, Bailey K. Ashford, Brooklyn

Rogers Marvel Architects

P.S. 196, Ten Eyck, Brooklyn
P.S. 380, John Wayne, Brooklyn
P.S. 9, Queens

Ronnette Riley Architect

P.S. 32, Belmont School, Bronx
P.S. 149, Sojourner Truth, Manhattan

Rockwell Group

P.S. 1, The Bergen School, Brooklyn
P.S. 5, Dr. Ronald McNair, Brooklyn
P.S. 17, Henry D. Woodworth, Brooklyn
P.S. 106, Edward Everett Hale, Brooklyn
P.S. 137, Rachel Jean Mitchell, Brooklyn
P.S. 145, Andrew Jackson, Brooklyn

Tod Williams Billie Tsien Architects

P.S. 1, Courtlandt, Bronx
P.S. 28, Wright Brothers, Manhattan
P.S. 101, Andrew Draper, Manhattan

Tsao & McKown Architects

P.S. 46, Edgar Allen Poe, Bronx
P.S. 86, Kings Bridge Heights, Bronx
P.S. 94, Kings College, Bronx
P.S. 246, Poe Center, Bronx
P.S. 19, Marino Jeantet School, Queens

Weiss Manfredi Architects

P.S. 42, R. Vernam School, Queens

Lonni Tanner
Founding Director, Robin Hood L!brary Initiative,
New York, New York

Henry Myerberg
Principal, HMA2 Architects,
New York, New York

CLIENT

The Robin Hood L!brary Initiative was conceived in 2001, a time when there was a lot of energy surrounding public schools in New York City. I had worked at the Robin Hood Foundation, a nonprofit focused on eradicating poverty in the city, for many years, and the organization convened an internal group to focus on education because we understood that literacy was intimately related to poverty. Externally, a new chancellor had just taken over the city's board of education, and a study had been released saying that good libraries had a direct effect on student performance. With those and many other things happening, we got to thinking about the role of libraries in the public schools. I visited about 100 elementary schools in the city to examine the state of their libraries, exploring really basic questions like: What are libraries? What do they mean to the people who use them? How are they integrated into the schools?

A lot of the places that I visited were in total disrepair. In other cases, there were rooms that said "Library" over the door, but there were no books inside, only empty shelves. This was not necessarily the fault of the schools; the budgets just weren't there. Often there was no money to hire full-time librarians, even though there was a mandate to have libraries in the elementary schools. When you started probing further and talking to the principals, there was a very serious disconnect. Everyone spoke with wonderful language about libraries, saying they were "the heart of the schools," but I wasn't seeing that. Rather than feeling despair at the situation, I saw it all as a great opportunity to transform these library spaces into vibrant places.

A couple of years earlier, I had worked with architect Henry Myerberg to design a library for one of the charter schools that Robin Hood was funding. That project was a great experience, so Henry was one of the first people I called. We decided to partner again and see what we could do a second time around. I also started running focus groups to learn more about what people—from teachers to principals to members of non-profits—thought of the libraries in the city's elementary schools. ▸

ARCHITECT

When Lonni Tanner from Robin Hood approached me to tackle this larger library project, one of the first things we did was conduct a series of workshops to think about the role the libraries would play in the future of the schools. This included a roundtable of people from Robin Hood, architects, teachers, and Harold O. Levy, who, at the time, was chancellor of the New York City Department of Education.

We began a pilot program, which became known as the L!brary Initiative, to transform ten school libraries. The mission focused on the measurable goal of boosting literacy and the immeasurable goal of instilling a love of learning in children. Studies show that children who have positive educational experiences in first through third grades have a better chance of succeeding thereafter. As much as design was an important aspect of this project, it was really an educational mission.

In one day, I made ten phone calls to ten architect friends. Nine of those ten firms signed on immediately. I pitched the project as an amazing opportunity and talked about the conditions in the school system. I told these architects, "Here's a chance for you to help invent ideas for what the school library can be." I think architects naturally are interested in doing creative work, and this ▸

Gluckman Mayner Architects
P.S. 189, Manhattan

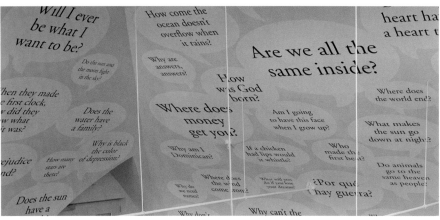

was a creative outlet. A lot of architects, too, are just interested in trying to make a difference in the world.

Having done a number of library projects myself, it was great to be involved in these early conversations because we were reconceiving what a library is. If you think back to 1999, it was a point in time when the idea of using computer systems to access library catalogues was still pretty new. The prevailing thought was that books and computers were like cowboys and farmers: There was no relationship between the two, but they are really quite complementary. Computers facilitate group work much more readily than books do. We developed a collaborative setting where computers, books, tables, and chairs were all movable and interchangeable.

For the first round of libraries, there were ten architecture firms involved, and each one was assigned to a school. The projects were located throughout the five boroughs, but they were all basically the same size, 2,000 square feet or so. We figured out that if the library held 10,000 books, it would be roughly big enough for two classes—one of younger kids and one of older kids—to use the space at once. The idea was always to make these spaces as flexible as possible. The ten architecture firms met on a regular basis to do pin-ups of their designs and share ideas for layouts and materials. It was an extraordinarily collaborative environment. ▸

After that, it became clear that better libraries were something the schools wanted, but turning the idea into a reality would be challenging. There was no money in the budget for that work, so I went out and enlisted people in advance of forming an actual program, to see if we could generate some excitement.

The first request I made was to Scholastic, the children's educational publisher, to ask for a million books. The company had donated 1,000 books to the library at the Beginning with Children Charter School, which Henry and I had done together. Scholastic said yes to my request, and that donation convinced me that the support was there for the program we would soon name the L!brary Initiative.

At the same time, Henry was working to enlist more architects. We knew that adding books and new carpet was not enough. Design would allow the project to become much more. The involvement of architects—particularly ones who were donating their time on a pro bono basis—attracted funders and gave me a carrot to bring to the schools and say, "We're doing something incredible here. Let's take the opportunity to elevate what a library can be and do."

Initially we were just going to work on a couple of libraries, but then donated materials started pouring in. In the end, we got more than two million books donated: one million from Scholastic, one million from HarperCollins, and hundreds of thousands from other publishers. You name it—everything from computers to carpet was donated. Syracuse University ended up offering librarians in the schools we worked with an opportunity to attend its masters program in library science for the price of an advanced degree from a local state university. And as more and more people got involved, the idea jumped from "Let's do a couple of libraries" to "Let's transform all public elementary school libraries in New York City."

We engaged more than seventy-five consultants at the beginning of the initiative; some of them donated their time for more than a year to make this thing fly. We simply needed that level of commitment to get the program off the ground. To the credit of the board of education, the chancellor agreed to give $10 million to the project right from the start. That was amazing. A lot of the designs helped spur the board to envision what these spaces could be. Without the designs, I don't think that would have happened.

We brought in Sciame Construction early on, which was key. The board usually teamed with contractors who were not accustomed to working with the kind of architects that we enlisted. We wanted the architects to be comfortable and have assurances that their designs would be built well, and Sciame has an excellent reputation and track record. Sciame donated all of its team's time for the first ten projects, and the architects got to focus on what they are good at: connecting ▷

top
Gluckman Mayner Architects
P.S. 192, Manhattan

middle and bottom
Rockwell Group
P.S. 106, Brooklyn

Once the libraries were assigned, everybody went out to meet with the librarian, principal, and teachers at his or her school. We all got to see the schools firsthand, to watch the kids coming into school and to observe some classes. Out of that, we got a sense of what the present experience was. It was community-activist work as much as it was architectural work; the architectural work was the tool driven by the social mission. The project always had that kind of heart, and it always captured everyone's emotional sides.

Our objective was that the new libraries shouldn't look like any other spaces in the schools. Many times, the schools we went into were pretty grim and looked like penitentiaries for eight-year-olds; there was nothing welcoming. We felt strongly that libraries are important, and they need to look important. Our other idea was that libraries aren't necessarily places where you always have to be quiet. We did not conceive of these as reading rooms. They're intended to be interactive places where students can prepare presentations, teachers can teach, volunteers can have story time for younger children. Our libraries are not places of quiet; they're spaces of communication.

The first public school that my firm at the time worked with was P.S. 50 in the Bronx. The director of that library had a vision of how the kids could relate to the space. He told us, "At the end of the school day, these kids ▷

have the choice to go to the playground or go hang out with their friends. I would like a bunch of them to say, 'Hey, after school, let's go to the library!'" After that, we made a real effort to engage the kids, even doing workshops with them. Lonni brought in a friend who taught the students poetry, and the kids' poems were stenciled in a frieze band in the library. Having their work as a permanent installation in the library was saying that the students were also part of the collections. We used design to instill pride. Maybe someone will come back to the library years from now and say, "Look, there's my name."

Later, when we worked on P.S. 106 in Brooklyn, we tried to transform a bunch of classrooms into a single library, but it was clear the air vents would make renovations problematic. We went to the top floor of the building and found that there was an abandoned attic space with a wonderful vaulted ceiling and windows with great views. That was the good news. The bad news was that the windows were so high the kids couldn't see out of them. There was an old desk positioned by a window, so the kids could climb up and see the skyline of Manhattan. It reminded me of something I had learned at a conference I'd gone to about children's services: Children are natural performers. And if you're a parent, you know that right away. In thinking about this, we came up with the idea of creating large steps, which would allow the kids to see the ▶

view and where they could climb and perform, as if it was a stage. On the ceiling, there are a series of questions posed by the kids to remind them that learning really begins with asking questions.

With Robin Hood, I've personally overseen a dozen libraries. Some of the simplest ideas were the most replicable and successful, like putting books on the perimeter of the room the way older, traditional libraries do, which creates room for kids to interact in the middle. One issue that was kind of funny was thinking about security systems. Most libraries have checkpoint security systems to protect the books, but there was some debate about that during the design phase. The systems are expensive, and we thought, in a kind of glib way, that if the kids kept the books longer than they should have, that wasn't the worst thing that could have happened. It would actually be a sign of success.

I credit Lonni for recognizing that the libraries needed to have great designs in order to attract donors. Furthermore, she realized that to get architects and designers to work pro bono you also need to allow them the opportunity to do creative work. The level of quality in these spaces is certainly the hallmark of what Robin Hood is all about. Lonni was good about bringing in outside support as well. Benjamin Moore and Scholastic were there from the very beginning. Harper Collins also donated ▶

with the clients and understanding the problems that needed to be to solved. We wanted to create libraries that brought people together, like a town hall within the school.

From the beginning, I wanted to involve the students in some part of the design process; that's where the graphic design firm Pentagram came in. Michael Beirut, one of the firm's partners, came up with a wonderful idea to put murals in the libraries. In those spaces in many of the schools, he and his team depicted the year's best or most-improved readers through cartoons, paintings, or photographs. In some cases, the students were involved in creating the murals. For instance, an Indian artist that we worked with had the kids make art with their feet, and he made it into a mural. Hundreds of kids came pouring into the library to participate.

For the children, the more innovation the better. They went bananas over the designs. Once a library was completed, I loved watching the students tiptoe in. They were afraid to touch anything. The rooms were brand new, and the kids didn't know what to make of them. It was just amazing to watch someone see something like this for the first time. These were imagination rooms, to be used not just for reading but also for art and theater. The first library designed by Tsao & McKown Architects even has a stage. The day after one of the spaces opened, one boy brought his clothes and other belongings to school because he wanted to live in the library.

The first library that Tod Williams Billie Tsien Architects designed was fascinating to me because the team suspended green canopies from the ceiling to create a sense of quiet, peace, and relaxation. When you pull up the shades, there's a sea of housing projects, so watching kids escape that environment and find a place to feel at home for an afternoon was pretty wonderful.

The designs helped drive other changes in the schools and even outside of them. We built an outdoor library, designed by landscape architect Ken Smith, at the second largest elementary school in the country, which is in Corona, Queens. Twenty-two hundred kids of seventy nationalities are represented in that one school. We even had a librarian conducting outdoor classes.

All told, the L!brary Initiative mobilized countless contributors and tens of millions of dollars in donated materials and services. It transformed fifty-six schools throughout New York's five boroughs, touching tens of thousands of kids. It's hard to imagine a more important space in a school than a library; every single kid goes there. By improving just 5 percent of a building's real estate, we were able to reach 100 percent of the students. In that and so many other respects, the L!brary Initiative is an incredibly powerful model.

books, and Apple helped out with some of the computer systems. Once the initiative became more publicly known, other funders also wanted to participate.

I would love the opportunity to chat with one of the students in ten years and ask, "Did this library change your life?" That's the part we don't know yet. I've always admired Andrew Carnegie, who funded more than 1,600 libraries across the country in the early twentieth century because he knew, from his own experience, what a difference it would make in people's lives. It didn't matter how many, just that it would make a difference to some. When you talk about education, you can't always use measurable devices to reflect a program's value. One thing I feel certain of is that, if you incorporate design, it helps signify how important a place is. It's true for Carnegie's libraries and those created by Robin Hood. And people take pride in that.

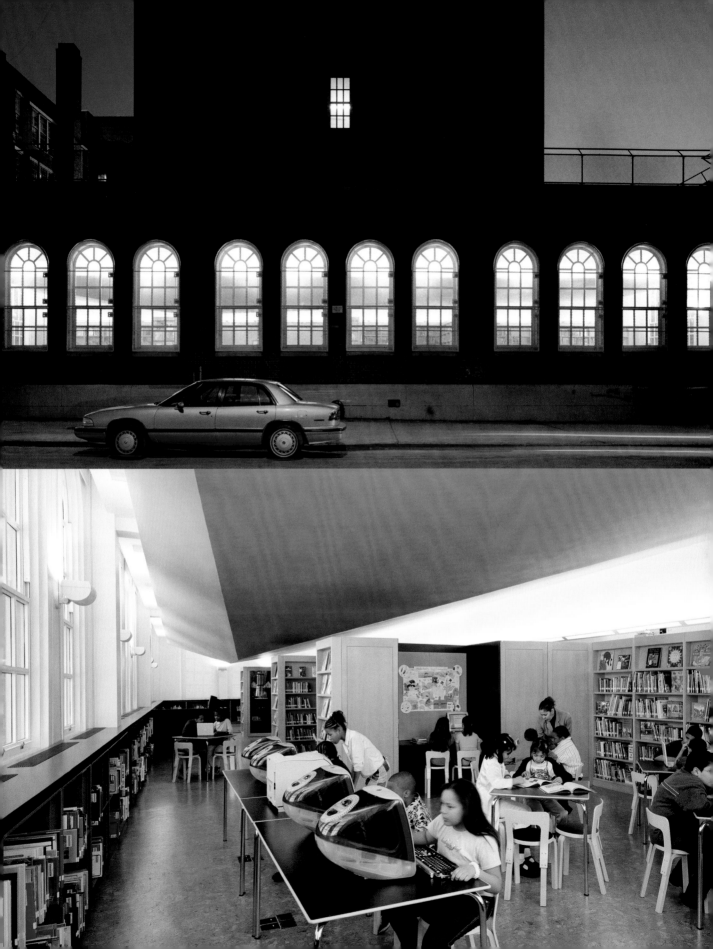

Outdoor Classroom

Outdoor Classroom at Eibs Pond Park
Location Staten Island, New York **Date** 2000 **Client** The Parks Council **Client liaison** Kate Chura **Design firm** Marpillero Pollak Architects **Design team** Marc Brossa, Gwynne Keathley, Jessica Levin, Amy Lin, Sandro Marpillero, Travis Merritt, Linda Pollak, Deanna Smith, Karen Tamir, Brett Thevenote, Sari Weissman **Area** 680 sq. ft. **Cost** $25,000 **Estimated value of pro bono design services** $18,000 **Websites** www.newyorkersforparks.org, www.mparchitectsnyc.com

Kate Chura
Former Director of Operations, The Parks Council,
New York, New York

CLIENT

During my tenure with the Parks Council (now called New Yorkers for Parks), we had a master plan to transform abandoned lots in specific neighborhoods throughout New York City into parks. To select the sites, we solicited proposals from neighborhood groups and worked with these groups to create public spaces that the community would, in turn, care for. I became the person to coordinate the designers, one of whom was Linda Pollak at Marpillero Pollak Architects.

Our site at Eibs Pond Park in Staten Island was a challenging location, surrounded by public housing and the Hubert H. Humphrey elementary school. City staff could not visualize the park beyond its run-down condition. They more or less said, "Those are the housing projects. Nobody cares. Why should we use our resources there?" At one meeting, they discussed planting vegetative screens around the buildings that bordered the park. I thought, "The reason nobody goes in the park is because they can't see into it!"

Another nonprofit, the Trust for Public Land, had preserved the area and later transferred the property to the New York City Department of Parks and Recreation, at which point the Parks Council started on the environmental remediation. The kettle ponds at Eibs Pond Park were formed when chunks of icebergs dropped off and landed there many thousands of years ago; the ponds are an important resource that, essentially, had been undeveloped. Throughout our work, the park was transformed from a scary, horrible place into an incredible natural resource, and the community understood the value of the site.

We wanted to design this project so that community members, including young people, could build much of it. Our vision was to divide construction into smaller processes, each of which would be a teaching experience. This allows more people to get involved. Tapping into the human resources in the community has a galvanizing effect on everyone. When the community is a part of a building project and is involved in every step of the design, clean up, installation, maintenance, and teaching—those spaces stay around a lot longer. ▸

Linda Pollak
Principal, Marpillero
Pollak Architects,
New York, New York

ARCHITECT

The Outdoor Classroom for Eibs Pond Park was the second of many pro bono projects in which my firm has participated. It was a wonderful process and allowed us to understand the potential in making targeted interventions in underserved urban areas.

I became involved in this project after serving as a juror for a design program run by the Parks Council. Before we became involved, the council had chosen the park as the project site and done some analysis and cleanup. Throughout its history, the site had been a dairy farm, golf club, prisoner of war camp, and, most recently, a dump. By the time we started, the council's team had hauled nineteen wrecked cars and more than 1,000 tires out of one of the ponds.

Eibs Pond Park is in a pretty tough neighborhood. The park is surrounded on two sides by large public housing projects. The nearby school's academic scores are at the bottom of those of the nearly 700 New York City primary schools. We worked with the science teachers there to site the classroom within a five-minute walk from the school, allowing for a round-trip visit within one class period. We put in an accessible path from the school to the edge of the park and a ramp from which you enter the classroom. This is a ▸

rich project. It is basically a very simple structure, but it enables you to access and value an environment.

Although our firm designed the classroom, a team of AmeriCorps volunteers did most of the building. We built giant, one-eighth-scale framing models in basswood to show the volunteers how the classrooms were put together. The Parks Council sourced sustainably forested redwood in 3-by-12-inch sections and other larger dimensions for the framing. The only cladding was a small portion of the roof and floor. My partner, Sandro Marpillero, went to the site once a week to see the building progress. It invariably would be built slightly differently than what we had intended, so he would make sketches to show the group how to turn the corner and get to the next step.

The classroom is a 24-foot-long floating pier with an open edge that engages the wetland edge. One side is porous to the view. I liked the idea of creating a "collector," a space where kids could gather specimens and samples, so we gave them lots of shelves to hold special rocks and other things. The classroom is next to a very beautiful birch tree on the bank of the pond, one of the few healthy, mature trees on the site. In the main gathering area, there is a bird wall: At a community event, we made birdhouses and put them on the wall next to the tree. Another wall has a planter box for native plantings. ▸

The wetland environment restricted the type of materials that we could use on the classroom structure. We wanted materials that would look good and hold up, but also be ecologically responsible, so we decided on environmentally certified redwood. Our next challenge was shipping the wood from California to New York. To make this financially feasible, the architects designed the classroom so all the wood could be delivered in one shipment.

In New York, people know the sign of a safe park: the presence of women and children. At Eibs Pond Park, we created pathways designed with vantage points, because people do not move through spaces when they can not see to the other side. Subsequently, women and children started traversing the park as a way to get from one point to another. This signaled to the community that it was safe.

Eibs Pond Park and its outdoor classroom are now destinations for the community. The classroom is striking, with walls made up of slats to let light through. One wall faces a magnificent birch tree a few feet away and has become a place for schoolkids to display birdhouses. When I first visited the nearby elementary school, you had to cross the parking lot and step over a guardrail to reach a path that led to the park. Now there is a clear, safe path to the park from the school and the street. That is a huge success. The park is a beautiful natural resource in a densely populated, urban area of New York City. Bridging those two very extreme worlds—the built world and the natural environment—was a great opportunity.

The classroom is elevated over the site to protect the wetland edge. There is a pier attached for walking out over the pond and fishing. The pier floats up and down, allowing you to perceive that the water levels are changing over the years. A portion of the deck has an open floor over the hydrologic soil, an area that floods and drains each year. From the edge of the classroom floor, you can see plants growing through the boards.

The outdoor classroom is now a destination. From the park edge, 300 feet away, you can see it. It strategically feels very open but still allows you to feel protected and enclosed. It is a social, urban space and a natural space. The degree to which a project like this can interpret and communicate the complexity of the urban and natural environments is transformative. This project was a chance to give a community access to nature once again.

Health

Adopt A Room
Minneapolis, Minnesota
Perkins+Will

Homeless Prenatal
San Francisco, California
Peterson Architects

Judson Center
Royal Oak, Michigan
Hathorne Architects

Planned Parenthood
San Francisco Bay Area, California
Fougeron Architecture

Virginia Garcia
McMinnville, Oregon
Scott | Edwards Architecture

YWCA
Chicago, Illinois
HOK

Adopt A Room

Adopt A Room
Location University of Minnesota Children's Hospital–Fairview, Minneapolis, Minnesota **Date** 2006 **Client** Adopt A Room Foundation **Client liaison** Brian Schepperle **Design firm** Perkins+Will **Design team** Sandy Christie, Chuck Knight, Elizabeth Rominski, John Spohn, Jerry Worrell **Area** 860 sq. ft. **Cost** Not available **Estimated value of pro bono design services** $130,000 **Websites** www.adoptaroom.org, www.perkinswill.com

John Spohn
Senior Associate,
Perkins+Will,
Minneapolis, Minnesota

ARCHITECT

Our work for the Adopt A Room Foundation began when two fathers who knew our managing principal, Chuck Knight, approached Perkins+Will. The fathers were friends who had each recently lost a child to a lifelong illness. They were somewhat dismayed by the conditions they and their children had endured at various hospitals, and they simply wanted to ensure that future patients didn't have the same experiences. Initially there was some discussion of just putting a large TV or a video-game system in the rooms and improving the furniture, but we realized a complete redesign was in order.

The University of Minnesota Children's Hospital-Fairview allowed us to take two semiprivate ▸

Brian Schepperle
Chair, Adopt A Room Foundation,
White Bear Lake, Minnesota

CLIENT

My family spent ten years in and out of hospitals caring for my daughter, who suffered from acute lymphoblastic leukemia. During our treatments in Southern California, the Midwest, and on the East Coast, we found the same thing: rooms that were small and not set up for long-term stays.

Sometimes our family would spend sixty continuous days in one room. We did everything possible to make it feel like home for our daughter. We literally bought a van so we could load up everything from her bedroom at our house—Barbie dolls, pictures, everything. We would always transform her stale little hospital rooms into special places that were just for her.

From our earliest visits to doctors and hospitals, I was always told that the attitude of patients played a very large role in how they felt and maybe even, to some degree, how they managed pain and healed. It instilled in me a belief that every effort we took to make the hospital room a home away from home mattered. The fact that she was comfortable there mattered.

After I lost my daughter, I started reflecting on the frustrations and shortcomings of the hospitals where we lived for years on end. I felt it would be a disservice to my daughter if everything I learned from watching her did not benefit other patients and families. No matter how good the care is, it's a very long experience. Fighting a disease is about more than the quality of care; it's also about environment. David Millington, who had also lost a child, and I founded the Adopt A Room Foundation on the belief that, while we can't control the illness, we can control the environment.

We enlisted architect Chuck Knight and his firm, Perkins+Will, to reconceive what a hospital room is, how it looks, and what it feels like. We did so by bringing together kids who were patients, their families, and a group of doctors, nurses, and researchers. There were about six kids in the initial design charrette, and all those kids are gone now, I think. We asked them what they wanted in these rooms, and we listened. Our goal was to think outside the box, with no budgets and no preconceptions. ▸

rooms and one private room and make them into two private rooms. The design process for the rooms was open to a number of people here in the Minneapolis office of Perkins+Will. Most of them had backgrounds in healthcare design and were eager to approach this project in a different manner than the standard work in that field.

As a part of our design charrette, we actually carved out a part of our office space to create a large-scale mock-up of a patient room. We did so to bring the children, their parents, and healthcare providers into our space and out of the environment they're accustomed to.

During the charrette, a lot of ideas surfaced, like installing double beds in the rooms so mothers or fathers could sleep comfortably rather than in a chair or on the floor. One child said, "I'd like to paint my room with color," which evolved into the design of an LED-based color-lighting system that was integrated into both of the rooms. The LEDs are programmed through interactive touch screens at the children's bedsides. They can change the color not only of the domed ceilings but of the entire rooms. A major goal was to give control back to the patient or the family and let them make the room a place where they are comfortable.

Parents were telling us that, while their child was hospitalized, they still had to do things like pay bills, work, and try to continue their own lives, so we designed a ▶

home-office area in the rooms, which has computers and Internet access. That's an example of a very simple, common-sense design element that addresses an important need of the parents and families.

We also thought about how families interact within a patient-care environment. One of the simplest ideas to come out of this was to include a table—like a kitchen table—in the rooms. A kitchen table is an important place where families congregate, eat, play cards, and do homework. We had access to all the technology in the world, but the adjustable-height, 36-inch round tables we put in the rooms are used more than anything; they restore a sense of normalcy. The family can slide the bed to the table, allowing two parents to share a dinner with their child. It is such a simple object that could be added to any patient room at a minimal cost. And that's the kind of design solutions we were looking for: small things that have big impacts.

Some of our ideas are already being replicated. The university has used the rooms as models in the design of a new children's hospital, which is being constructed just across the river. We did not design the facility, unfortunately, but the architects looked at our rooms and incorporated aspects of them.

This project has been widely circulated around Perkins+Will's other offices across the country. ▶

Everyone throughout the firm is familiar with it. I'm usually the one who goes out and talks to different groups, sharing some of the thoughts and ideas we had when we designed these rooms. This was fundamentally different than any other project that I've been associated with. Because we were hired by Adopt A Room and not by a health-care organization or the facility, we had a different client, and we kind of marched to a different band. That was one of the reasons why I think the project ended up where it did rather than as a more traditional design.

Ultimately, the idea of Adopt A Room is to get corporations, foundations, and donors to rally around the redesign of hospital rooms in their communities. We offer up our two rooms as models, and we hope others will emerge.

The kids talked about really basic stuff, like having trouble getting in and out of the tubs. Many children's hospitals have child-sized tubs in the rooms, but sometimes the kids can't even lift their legs to get in them, so we decided to install showers. The kids also raised the point that the bathroom and bathtub floors were very cold, so we incorporated radiant-heat floors in the new rooms. Radiant-heat floors sound like a luxurious amenity; however, when an immunosuppressed child takes a shower, stagnant water is like a petri dish for bacteria. The heated floors evaporate water at a faster rate and dry the floor, so it's less likely to trap bacteria and cause infections. The idea was a great coming together of the doctors, patients, and architects. The doctors and the researchers were particularly receptive to it because their goal is to keep infections down and keep the rooms as clean and sterile as possible.

One child, whom we lost, said, "I spend a lot of time on my back, and I can't look out the window." That statement made us wonder how hospital rooms could make better use of their ceilings, which are usually made of dropped panels. We ultimately included a giant dome that covers three-quarters of the ceiling. When children are on their backs and can't sit up or if they are immobilized in any way, they can choose the imagery projected on the dome. At night, it can be a constellation of stars or even pictures of their homes. We did that just to give a kid who can't look out a window a sense of control and something to look at to spark her imagination.

We started Adopt A Room with a question: Wouldn't it be great to design a hospital room that kids didn't mind going to? Having been in countless hospital rooms over more than a decade, it almost seemed like an unattainable goal. But that's exactly what we accomplished.

Homeless Prenatal

John Peterson
Principal, Peterson
Architects,
San Francisco, California

Homeless Prenatal Program
Location San Francisco, California **Date** 2005 **Client** Homeless Prenatal Program **Client liaison**
Martha Ryan **Design firm** Peterson Architects **Design team** Arlene Lee, John Peterson **Area** 26,800 sq. ft.
Cost $4.65 million **Estimated value of pro bono design services** $120,000 **Websites**
www.homelessprenatal.org, www.petersonarch.com

Martha Ryan
Founder and Executive Director, Homeless Prenatal Program,
San Francisco, California

ARCHITECT

Since its inception in the early 1990s, my firm, Peterson Architects, has always done a great deal of pro bono work. In addition to founding and providing work space for Public Architecture for many years, we have worked with a range of nonprofit groups, from arts organizations and community development corporations to social-service agencies like Homeless Prenatal Program. We became involved with Homeless Prenatal when one of its board members approached us and asked us to design a new building for a piece of property that the organization had purchased. The lot was small, which meant that the building would have to be quite tall to accommodate the group's space needs. Because the building was also on fill, it called for a very deep foundation, which itself is always a costly endeavor.

Homeless Prenatal had purchased the property near the peak of the dot-com era in the late '90s, but the real estate market had softened significantly by the time the organization was prepared to build. It became clear that the cost to build from the ground up would be much greater. Meanwhile countless dot-coms had gone out of business, leaving a solid inventory of vacant buildings in the South of Market neighborhood and other parts of San Francisco. So, after an assessment, Peterson Architects and HPP board president David Prowler developed a proposal for ▷

CLIENT

When the dot-com era hit San Francisco, our board and staff knew we were at risk. We were working on three floors of a fifteen-story building, and the dot-coms were swallowing up space while offering four times the rent that nonprofits like us were paying. We knew we had to move, and we wanted to be in charge of our own destiny.

Our search for a new space was a multiyear journey and involved buying another piece of property before finding our current home. Our board president, David Prowler, had worked with John Peterson of Peterson Architects, who quickly assessed our situation and counseled our board out of using the property that we had purchased. He then very graciously agreed to come with us every time we looked at another building that we thought we might be serious about. John would walk through the space and give a nod or talk about it afterward. He never really said, "Do it" or "Don't do it." He just objectively told us what it would take to make it work for us. The beauty of John was that he saw things that we didn't see, so his feedback was very important.

John really got to know what we wanted and needed as we toured more and more buildings and I talked about the different services that we wanted to add. It was like an on-the-job training program for John and for us. He also learned by spending time in our old space, and he got to know us personally. Thus, when Homeless Prenatal found a building and went to hire an architect, we dutifully interviewed many different firms, but it was a no-brainer to go with Peterson Architects. We knew that John was the right guy because of his pro bono service, the attention he paid to us, and the support that he gave us until we finally bought this property. For two years, every time we looked at a building, John was there—and we looked at a lot of buildings.

The structure we ultimately decided to buy cost $4.65 million. It had been set up as a "dot-com incubator," with a lot of small, private offices on the main floor. As you go up, the spaces become bigger and bigger. It also had parking downstairs. The building was pretty much built out, so we really just renovated it. After the purchase, we didn't have a lot of money to spend on renovations, so we didn't tear down a ton of walls; instead, we made the space work for us. That's exactly what Peterson Architects helped us do. ▷

Homeless Prenatal to sell the property, and we pledged to help the staff find a new space. The board of directors ultimately agreed to the sale and to use the money to buy an existing building, even though one hadn't been identified yet. Together we embarked on a journey to find a new structure, looking at numerous properties and conducting in-depth "test-and-fit" studies for a handful of them, including the one that would become the organization's new home.

After finding a new building, we went through the acquisition process with Homeless Prenatal. At that point, my firm could not financially support doing the rest of the work pro bono, so it was a perfect moment for the group to transition to another firm. Instead they chose to retain our firm because we had demonstrated our commitment to the Homeless Prenatal mission. The team saw us make decisions that improved the organization.

Our biggest design challenge was to make the most of Homeless Prenatal's very limited resources. One could argue that we provided high-quality design, even though the facility was less ideal design-wise than if we had created a new building from the ground up. Homeless Prenatal understood that the advantages and opportunities associated with this new space outweighed those of a new building in terms of efficiency, return on investment, and schedule (since the staff could move in quicker). The new ▶

building had the added bonus of extra space that the organization could rent out to generate income. Overall the cost savings were staggering, and the staff ended up getting something like twice the amount of space for less money than it would have cost to develop their previous parcel. We would have failed, I think, as design professionals if we passed up this opportunity and designed a new building.

Homeless Prenatal's previous leased space spanned three floors in a mid-rise building on Market Street in downtown San Francisco. It was a sort of rabbit warren of rooms—quite confusing and disorienting. There was absolutely no cohesion of space or sense of community. When the organization moved into its new building, the group immediately saw improvements across the board in the areas of staff comfort, happiness, and enthusiasm, as well as client satisfaction. They also saw a spike in funding, a significant portion of which was attributed to the new facility. There is a sense of optimism and success that the new space has brought to the organization.

Months after we completed our work, Martha Ryan, the founder and executive director of Homeless Prenatal, told me a story. The organization had a long-term funder who had given on the order of $30,000 annually. The funder came for a visit to the new facility, walked around, and liked it very much. That person called the next day and said, "Please make ▸

I started this program working only with pregnant homeless women, but very early on, I realized that prenatal care alone was not enough. We really needed to provide services that help families remain healthy and help them create an environment where their children can thrive. The location of our new space is fantastic and so much more suitable for our clientele. Our former facility's location at Sixth and Market Streets is what I would call "ground zero" for drug dealers. Clients would come to us, and they would be struggling to get into recovery, or they would have children with them. They would go out of our building and they'd get accosted by people who wanted to sell them drugs or who knew them before. It just wasn't a safe place. Our new building is five blocks from San Francisco General Hospital, major bus lines have stops close by, and we don't have any problems with drug dealing. In fact, there's an undercover police station right across the street.

In our old space, we also had a very small waiting area. People who come to us for services are often extremely stressed out, and there would be lots of fights as a result of that combination. In our new home, we designed a very open and welcoming double-height reception area. Officers from charitable foundations and individual donors regularly come in and see the beautiful space, and they're sold. They see our ability to provide a continuum of services that helps families who are in crisis and in search of help and a new beginning.

In many cases, when nonprofits are serving poor and homeless people, they have dingy spaces that feel like they're underground. Conversely, our building is open and welcoming. We went from having 10,000 square feet to 26,800 square feet, which enabled us to bring in other groups to offer services we don't provide ourselves. For example, the midwives at San Francisco General come here to do group prenatal care. We're also now doing free tax preparation for the working poor, and we have therapists from San Francisco General Hospital's trauma center come here. We offer a true continuum of services, but, overall, this building is now one of our best tools to help women and families exit poverty and homelessness.

your application this year for ten times the historic amount." To be clear, that donor was so convinced by what she saw that she increased Homeless Prenatal's funding tenfold. Martha firmly believes it was due to the design of the new facility.

Judson Center

Judson Center Autism Connections

Location Royal Oak, Michigan **Date** 2009 **Client** Judson Center **Client liaison** Stephanie Harlan
Design firm Hathorne Architects **Design team** Jessie Chen, Lars Graebner, Christina Hansen, Matt Hathorne
Area 5,000 sq. ft. **Cost** $750,000 **Estimated value of pro bono design services** $18,000 **Websites**
www.judsoncenter.org, www.hathorne-architects.com

Matt Hathorne
Principal, Hathorne
Architects,
Detroit, Michigan

ARCHITECT

The first thing I did when I started my own firm was place an ad offering free schematic design services in a publication produced by the Michigan Non-profit Association. After several phone calls from organizations that were not entirely committed to building, I heard from the Judson Center, offering me this opportunity.

Other than a few drawings for Habitat for Humanity, I had not worked on a pro bono basis as an architect prior to this project. In addition, this was the first project of any kind that my firm took on. I would like to say that my intentions for performing pro bono work were purely altruistic, but that is not entirely true. I saw offering design services to a nonprofit as a great way to establish myself while helping an organization keep its costs down.

Long before the project went into construction, a large team from the ▶

Stephanie Harlan
Director of Autism Connections, Judson Center,
Royal Oak, Michigan

CLIENT

Autism Connection's mission is to create a suitable atmosphere for children with autism and their families, providing them with a space where they can feel comfortable to be themselves. When we met Matt Hathorne of Hathorne Architects, it felt like a good philosophical match in terms of how he envisioned our project progressing. Autism Connections occupies a wing in the Judson Center, a nonprofit that helps improve the lives of families with special circumstances. In addition to autism services, that includes assisting adults with disabilities and families dealing with foster care and adoption.

Frankly, the interior of our former space was boring, and it didn't address our needs. Matt was very interested in designing a space that wasn't sterile like a doctor's office or institutional like a school building. He wanted it to feel like a welcoming community facility, a place you want to visit.

Matt tried to learn as much as he could about autism and did a lot of independent research. He frequently came in to work with us and watch the kids interact. We wanted to show him what it was like to work with these kids, who have many sensory challenges and behavioral issues. Matt even came to our summer program, which we hold off-site. Just from being there for one day, he came up with so many ideas.

One of the things he observed is that when kids with autism get overwhelmed by noises and lights, they will find a small, quiet space where they can remove themselves from all the craziness. At the summer camp, we took tables and put blankets over them so that the kids could have their own little safe spaces. Matt saw that and it gave him the idea of building hideaway nooks into the walls of our classrooms. The nooks give the kids a place to get away from the stimuli but still remain with the group. It is something unique about our therapy rooms. ▶

184   The Power of Pro Bono

Judson Center met with my colleague Lars Graebner and me on a weekly basis. We discussed the program and the space endlessly. I have never met a client so intent on getting it right. Obviously, concern over the sensitivity and special needs of the autistic children served as the catalyst for these discussions. Although I was given a lot of leeway on the design, the owner focused more on the user's comfort.

If you research autism, you find some very practical dos and don'ts for design, which, although helpful, are no substitute for having direct experience inform the design process. As the director of the center, Stephanie Harlan was able to quickly evaluate the implications of our decisions. We also walked through her classes and, together, developed some interesting ideas for the program. In a typical project, researching the program is incidental or done far in advance. In this case, continual research was critical to the design process.

The biggest success for me is that the space feels more like a community center than a clinic. I always felt like we were designing for three users: our client working in this space, the children using the space, and the parents. It was very important that the parents feel the center was a destination rather than a necessary burden. I didn't want them to have the impression they were dropping their kids off at a front desk to be walked down a lonely, narrow corridor to a door in a wall. ▸

The key to creating a communal feeling is to provide a generous space that pulls in as many people and functions as possible. Space and visibility are critical. For this reason, we lowered the walls to 6 feet and lifted the ceiling as high as possible within the existing construction. Introducing skylights permitted natural light to enter these rooms and unified the individual spaces under the vaulted ceiling.

The spaces between the classrooms contain services such as a library, computer room, and kitchen. All of these functions and the classrooms come together under this one ceiling because users can see past the lowered walls. In this way, everyone sees that they are sharing the space. The classroom walls are curved, which adds to the visual and physical fluidity. It is easy to keep an eye on the children and for the children to see around the corners. It also gives the user permission to move about the space freely.

One of the criteria for this project was to reduce noise travel. Wood-slat walls are often utilized in large auditoriums to break up and reduce noise. We applied this principle to the ceiling. Additionally, the curvature of the ceiling and the extension of the slats down the wall reduce the datum reference for the ceiling. These features make the space feel more organic, similar to being under a sky filled with white clouds. If you stretch your imagination, the skylights are gaps in the clouds where light penetrates. ▶

Matt also noticed that there are a lot of safety issues for kids with autism. They like to run, especially in circles. All the walls here have rounded edges instead of sharp corners, so that if the kids run into them, they won't hurt themselves. We also put fabric on the edges of the walls to create a sensory experience for the kids. The wooden slats on the walls also receive a lot of attention. The kids like to trace their hands along the lines up the walls; the verticality helps them feel organized. We educated Matt about the children's needs, and with all of these design features, he figured out a way to build solutions into the environment.

Our old space was comprised of modular office cubicles. There was a big, long hallway with conference rooms in the center and rows of cubicles on the edges. The color scheme was gray and drab, and there wasn't much natural light. It wasn't a welcoming environment for people with autism—or anybody, really. All of that was completely gutted and changed. Lighting was one of the key focuses of the design. Matt added skylights and a full wall of windows, which opened everything up.

Everything here is unique. I've never seen a building that has these modular pods, as we call them, for the therapy rooms. It's very creative and a wonderful use of the space that we had. The slatted ceiling is beautiful and makes the place look so big and airy; it throws the natural sunlight beautifully. I'm really proud of those features.

The staff absolutely loves the space. Anything would have been an improvement on what we had before, but this is wonderful. In our old space, we were apologetic. We'd say, "Sorry, it will be better someday." Now we're very proud to have people come to this beautiful, state-of-the-art facility, and to have a comfortable waiting area as well as suitable therapy space to help our kids. The staff was involved in all aspects of planning, so everybody takes some pride in the finished product. We were able to see the problems, find solutions, and actually create something that works for us. It was a really fun process.

I think we've gotten into Matt's heart a little bit. He definitely has a soft spot for the kids. He'll drop in and play with them and look at how the space is being used. He has stayed very involved in this project. The parents are thrilled when they walk in here, and the kids love coming here. To them, the space has become a big playground.

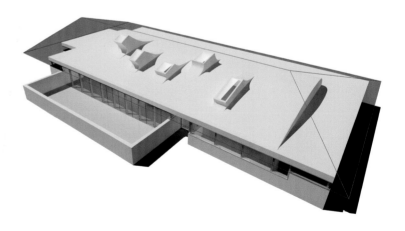

We are proud of these design elements, but I am probably most satisfied to see the parents and children congregate and use the space as a community center. This has been a very positive experience for me, and I plan on doing many more projects like it.

Planned Parenthood

Planned Parenthood Golden Gate
Location San Francisco Bay Area, California **Date** 1996–present **Client** Planned Parenthood Golden Gate
Client liaison Therese Wilson **Design firm** Fougeron Architecture **Estimated value of pro bono design services** Not available **Websites** www.ppgg.org, www.fougeron.com

Eastmont Health Center
Oakland, California
Clinic

**Good Samaritan
San Francisco**
San Francisco, California
Satellite site

Hayward Health Center
Hayward, California
Clinic

MacArthur Health Center
Oakland, California
Administrative offices, clinic

Maternity Waiting Village
Hosanna, Ethiopia
Master plan

Novato Health Center
Novato, California
Clinic, teen wellness center

**Roberts Women's
Health Center**
Redwood City, California
Clinic

Rohnert Park Health Center
Rohnert Park, California
Clinic

San Francisco Health Center
San Francisco, California
Administrative offices, clinic,
executive administrative offices

San Mateo Health Center
San Mateo, California
Administrative offices, call center,
clinic

San Rafael Health Center
San Rafael, California
Administrative offices, clinic

Santa Rosa Health Center
Santa Rosa, California
Clinic feasibility study

Anne Fougeron
Principal, Fougeron
Architecture,
San Francisco, California

ARCHITECT

My relationship with Planned Parenthood started in the 1990s at a time when there was violence against doctors who performed abortions. Those stories prompted Topher Delaney, my office partner at the time, and me to offer services to the organization. We started answering phones and doing whatever was needed, but when the staff found out I was an architect, they asked if I could help do some security upgrades on the San Francisco affiliate's four clinics. I agreed, even though I knew nothing about security design. Planned Parenthood had no background on the subject either. The organization was just starting to think about how to deal with the problem. Resources were being communicated from all the other affiliates, but everyone had a slightly different take on the matter. To educate myself on security, I used every resource and person I knew.

From the beginning, it was critical to me that the design for each facility make visitors feel like they are entering a very secure environment, but not one that's prison-like. We wanted the first impression to be pleasant, so the security features ▸

Therese Wilson
Executive Vice President, Planned Parenthood Golden Gate,
San Francisco, California

CLIENT

It all started with a fateful day in 1994 in Brookline, Massachusetts. A lone gunman went into a clinic that provided abortions. Then he went to the Planned Parenthood on the same street and opened fire, fatally shooting two staff members and wounding five people, including a security guard, volunteers, and clients. It was just horrific—and a real turning point in our work.

We had been dealing with a lot of protest activity and an abundance of violence against physicians, but nothing this severe. The shooting happened inside the health center and put everybody at risk: our staff, volunteers, patients, and, clearly, our physicians. In the old days, clients came in the door and met with us face-to-face. After the shooting, that had to change.

We had a forbidding task: figure out how to secure our facilities, yet at the same time, offer welcoming environments where we could have private and confidential discussions with our clients regarding very personal healthcare matters. We at Planned Parenthood pride ourselves on our relationships with patients and clients. We deal with very sensitive issues that revolve around sexual activity. We ensure confidentiality and privacy in our work.

In 1996, Planned Parenthood San Francisco merged with the larger regional affiliate, Planned Parenthood Golden Gate, creating a network of fourteen facilities across the Bay Area. At the four sites managed by Planned Parenthood San Francisco, we were absolutely stumped about how to proceed. Security was not our specialty, and we had no idea how to approach the task at hand. We did not have abundant resources or money to throw at the problem, but we knew it would be incredibly helpful to have a skilled architect help us start the conversation about how to approach the security issue at those locations. That is how our relationship with Anne Fougeron started. It was a crisis situation, and we needed the guiding force of someone like Anne. ▸

are not the first thing that the clients notice. Rather than buying premanufactured security systems, we custom designed a bullet-resistant steel window to fit into the walls. All of the bullet-resistant elements are completely hidden, and the use of interesting materials and colors disguise the fact that there's a barrier between visitors and staff.

After completing those upgrades, we made an inventory for each clinic, noting what was very urgent, what needed to be fixed soon, and what could wait. The document changed frequently as the organization got rid of clinics and aggregated others. In many of the facilities, the paint was terrible and parts of the infrastructure were crumbling and not working well. Some of the work was not glorious; we upgraded finishes and changed flooring. In some cases, however, the clinics needed to be remodeled with a fresh approach so that the organization could look and function better.

My firm has a strong interest in the materiality of architecture, so we created a prototypical palette of materials for Planned Parenthood. Materials were chosen for cost-effectiveness and longevity. With a palette, it's much easier to spend money on the right things: tested products that work. We also developed interchangeable furniture, so throughout the clinics, spaces can be made bigger or smaller by adding or subtracting pieces. ▸

Our first step with Anne was to secure the reception areas and waiting rooms at our sites and come up with a system to screen clients and bring them into the facilities through different levels of security. The work mostly was about incorporating bullet-resistant materials into our buildings without being too obvious. Anne offered solutions that worked for our spaces, and through that process, Planned Parenthood renovated old sites and constructed new sites, including a couple of full-scale health centers. Anne became our go-to person on each of those projects.

Planned Parenthood has completed a variety of projects with Anne, and in a way, the large ones are easier. When you're working from scratch, you don't have to, for example, squeeze an ADA-approved bathroom into an existing site or work around other parameters. All of the projects aim for efficiency in terms of the flow of clients and staff through the facilities. Now that we have designed some of the spaces together and have learned from each project, the process is down to a science.

One of my favorite projects is the Eastmont Health Center, which is in a crime-ridden neighborhood of East Oakland. About ten years ago, the office moved from a tiny, hodgepodge, old building adjacent to a mall to a site inside the mall. The developers wanted to turn the mall into a social-services hub and invited us to move in. We made the clinic safe and secure, using bullet-resistant glass and great signage, but it's also beautiful. I was there recently, and the exam rooms still look clean and fantastic; I am so happy that it looks like it did when we moved in.

When the Eastmont clinic opened, a client whom we had served in the old location came in. She marveled at the new space and couldn't believe that it was the same people and the same services—we looked completely different. She was overwhelmed by what Planned Parenthood had done for her as a patient and what the organization continually does as a healthcare provider for people like her. Planned Parenthood is committed to providing the greatest level of healthcare for low-income families and women. The emotion that the client felt is the best compliment Planned Parenthood could get.

In all of our sites, Anne understands that Planned Parenthood cannot be extravagant. She uses natural light to create a work environment that's pleasant for the staff and clients. She chooses bright paint colors to make spaces pretty and not sterile, like many healthcare environments. Anne, along with Planned Parenthood, is also committed to using sustainable materials. She has introduced us to some materials that really last, like cork flooring, which I love. Cork is sustainable, but it also needs no maintenance—a big win-win for us. Thousands of people come through our sites every month. There is a lot of wear and tear on the floors, but the cork holds up and still looks good.

Recently I was at our MacArthur site, which is our newest clinic designed by Anne. It's a beautiful facility with tons of skylights and natural light and a big, well-organized reception area. It is a really wonderful place to work. It's also a great example of working out a difference of opinion. I can look around the space and see bits and pieces that I remember working on in the design phase that turned out really nicely. During the design process, I argued the need for an additional bathroom to take the place of a proposed light well. Anne said, "No way! We're going to put the light well there." She and I sparred back and forth. I laugh about it now, because the light well is such an essential design feature of the building. It looks great and adds to the overall sense of calmness and beauty of the space. ▸

Over our fifteen-year partnership with Planned Parenthood, Fougeron Architecture has fully renovated two clinics in Oakland—MacArthur, which we worked on twice, and Eastmont. We have also done a lot of work on facilities on Eddy Street in San Francisco and in San Rafael and Hayward, California. We've redone five clinics total, some needing more design than others. A few facilities badly needed upgrading, including MacArthur, where we took the building down to the bare studs and started over.

As part of our commitment to the organization, we perform feasibility studies for potential new clinics as Planned Parenthood evaluates its various holdings and real estate. We have also worked on Planned Parenthood Golden Gates's administrative offices, executive office, and new call center. We help with small things, too, like moving offices, determining furniture needs, maintaining roofs, and installing skylights. We are on call whenever Planned Parenthood needs something. As the group's needs keep changing, we accommodate them.

Design is a priority for the sites, when feasible. The organization serves financially challenged people, but that's not the way the facilities should look. By providing the best service and environments possible, Planned Parenthood is more competitive in the healthcare field. The organization understands that when environments are nice, clients and staff appreciate them, and everyone gets along ▸

better. Design matters to everyone up to Planned Parenthood's senior executives; they understand its value and the recognition the organization gets for great-looking spaces.

It would be hard to put a value on all the pro bono services we've given Planned Parenthood. Off the top of my head, I would estimate we've donated between $6 million and $8 million worth of construction work, fees, and bidding. But, through our work with the organization, we were introduced to healthcare design, and now we are able to do larger healthcare projects. Our firm has won design awards for both the MacArthur and Eastmont facilities, which is a big part of our overall marketing strategy. The arrangement has been very successful for us.

Some of the subcontractors on the Planned Parenthood sites—many of whom are our usual vendors, such as Interface and Knoll—also have discounted their fees for the projects. For example, Interface gave us carpet that was valued at $25,000 and had been rejected by another job. Steelcase called one day and said that it had 100 chairs and would sell them to us at cost. Stuff like this happens all the time. We get discounts and help with different things. Every time we start a new job, we milk these contributions for all we can to see if anyone has leftover stuff that we can roll over. People see our work for Planned Parenthood and want to be a part of it. They often call me because they know I work with the organization. ▸

Sometimes the best job isn't the one with the biggest budget or the simplest process. Working with an organization like Planned Parenthood feeds the soul. It's important for designers to find these types of endeavors. We need it, or at least, I need it. For the office and my staff, this work shows a totally different side of the business, but we handle all the jobs the same way and with the same requirements. My staff understands that Planned Parenthood has a political and social agenda that matters to me and the office. Nobody is going to work for me if they don't believe in the organization's mission; it would be a terrible conflict. This work makes a big difference in how we think of ourselves in the world.

A few clients have been uncomfortable with our ties to Planned Parenthood, but they can choose to work with us or not. I am not going to pretend that I don't do this work. I am proud of it, and it's part of who I am. I originally volunteered for the organization because I was a woman who was seeing my reproductive rights challenged. I have a daughter, who at the time was five years old. I couldn't imagine a world where she would have more limited reproductive rights than I did. I could have worked pro bono for other organizations; this was a political decision. It is the greatest feeling to have found a client like Planned Parenthood, because I completely believe in the political agenda.

Planned Parenthood Golden Gate now serves as a resource for many of our affiliates across the country when they are undergoing big construction projects. They call us because of something they have seen or heard, and they're interested in using design to bring in clients. Design is definitely an important part of attracting clients and providing exceptional care. We have more return clients because they feel comfortable in our spaces.

Planned Parenthood Golden Gate's relationship with Anne is ongoing. We call her the "Agency Architect." We are so satisfied with her work, and she has a depth of knowledge about healthcare spaces, our specific requirements, and our work. I don't need to go reinvent that wheel with anybody else. Anne's staff also treats us like a high-paying customer. Often on pro bono projects, your work gets pushed to the bottom of the heap because of the needs of paying clients. Fougeron Architecture has never done that to us. As a leader of her team, Anne clearly sets the example for her staff.

The added value of working with an architect is immeasurable to our organization. It opened up other aspects of our work that may have gone unnoticed otherwise. If the crisis and tragedy that Planned Parenthood went through had any silver lining, it's that it got us thinking about design and spaces and how to provide healthcare in a different way that still retains the valuable interaction and relationship with our clients.

pages 194–95
clockwise from top left
MacArthur Health Center, Oakland;
Eastmont Health Center, Oakland;
Eastmont Health Center;
Eastmont Health Center;
San Mateo Health Center;
MacArthur Health Center;
San Francisco Health Center;
San Francisco Health Center;
San Mateo Health Center;
Eastmont Health Center

opposite top
San Mateo Health Center

opposite bottom
MacArthur Health Center, Oakland

Virginia Garcia

Virginia Garcia McMinnville Clinic
Location McMinnville, Oregon **Date** 2006 **Client** Virginia Garcia Memorial Health Center **Client liaison**
Gil Muñoz **Design firm** Scott | Edwards Architecture **Design team** Joan Jasper, Alden Kasiewicz, Sid Scott
Area 13,500 sq. ft. **Cost** $2.1 million **Estimated value of pro bono design services** $30,000 **Websites**
www.virginiagarcia.org, www.seallp.com

Gil Muñoz
CEO, Virginia Garcia Memorial Health Center,
Hillsboro, Oregon

CLIENT

Over the ten years that we have worked together, Scott | Edwards Architecture has sat down with us time and time again to understand our services and the population that we serve. Our organization, Virginia Garcia Memorial Health Center, is named after six-year-old Virginia Garcia, who, in 1975, traveled from Texas to Oregon with her parents in their search for farm work. Along the way, she cut her foot. Due to economic and language barriers, she never received medical care, and the resulting infection killed her. The center was formed to ensure that such situations are prevented in our community, and we now run a group of health facilities that provides services to uninsured and low-income communities in Washington and Yamhill Counties in Oregon. Our services are focused on primary care, dental health, behavioral health, pharmacies, and health education. We also provide outreach to the local population of farm workers, particularly in the summer months of the harvest season.

Scott | Edwards has helped us realize the potential in the spaces we have, like in the McMinnville facility, where we only had 1 acre of land. The architects knew the city and county zoning requirements for things such as parking, so they helped us pack as much as possible into the site's footprint. They also looked at the adjacencies of our services—for example, how dental interfaces with medical—to see how those would fit in with the lab and pharmacy services in the building. They consistently do a good job of helping us think through all of these different relationships. In the case of this project, Scott | Edwards looked at our available resources, both funding and spatial, and came up with a great design and a facility that really works for us from an operational standpoint.

Cost is always an issue for us. One of the things that we did with the McMinnville center was to have a combination of built-in casework and modular furnishings. That provides us the flexibility we need to make adjustments as we extend our services. Scott | Edwards worked closely with the contractor to look at how the engineering of some parts of the building could be done most cost effectively. As a nonprofit, we often cannot afford that level of attention. ▸

Joan Jasper and Sid Scott
Project Architect and
Principal, Scott | Edwards
Architecture,
Portland, Oregon

ARCHITECT

When we started our firm, in 1997, the Virginia Garcia Memorial Health Center was our first client, and we've been working with the nonprofit ever since. At that time, the center was constructing a new dental facility, the first new building it had ever put up. The organization had started by providing medical services in a refurbished garage, expanded into a house, and then put an addition on the house. It was that kind of growth. Since then, we've done about ten projects with Virginia Garcia, ranging from redoing the reception desk to building the first new ground-up clinic in McMinnville.

In most of our pro bono projects, our investment is up front. For example, we help clients figure out strategies to find funding. In order to be successful in fund-raising, we always need to put together a compelling story about the identity of the nonprofit and the role it plays in the community. About 20 percent of the work our firm does has some connection to either ▸

migrant farm workers or the Latino community. When we started out with the Virginia Garcia dental clinic, we wanted to understand more about the identity of the center's patients, so we visited a migrant camp, and that was quite an eye-opener for us. This particular group of folks really need help, basic amenities that we as architects are trained to provide.

Before we built the new facility, the McMinnville clinic was located in an old insurance agency's office. The place had about a quarter of the necessary space for a standard clinic, including four people sharing one office. We knew we had to do something, and so we worked with the leadership on how to start finding funding and a site. It was really interesting because the staff had gotten so used to working with the space they had, but it didn't serve them well at all.

In the new facility, we wanted to make sure that everywhere you looked you could see outside, and anytime you walked down a hallway there was natural light at its end. Initially we thought that was going to be impossible because of the limitations of the site, but it really became a nice organizing element to the building.

The biggest challenge was the size of the lot and what the client wanted to put on it. The staff wanted, and arguably needed, more square footage than we could build. We think that the end result was incredible, and the ▸

design came from the Virginia Garcia team as well as us. We engaged in a very collaborative process with the staff to fit 60,000 square feet of program into a 13,500-square-foot facility.

We've learned over time that, while nonprofits are very passionate about what they do, they're not in their fields to be developers. For them, it is all about the services they can provide. It's a good angle for us to help those types of clients with the infrastructures to make their operations as streamlined as possible. We're really big on making sure the organizations not only get the money they need to build or remodel, but that they also have the reserves to keep and maintain ▸

We are the only provider of primary care services for uninsured and low-income households in this area, so the McMinnville clinic has been embraced by the community. The city of McMinnville was also a real champion of this project and worked with us to secure grants. Through our partnership with the city, we were able to secure $600,000 in community-development funding. That provided enough equity for the project to move forward.

This facility has greatly increased our ability to provide high-quality services to the community. We didn't have dental services or a pharmacy before opening the new building, and now we do. Our behavioral health services were not very well integrated into our larger program, and now that is becoming a significant part of our mission.

The McMinnville space is pleasant to spend time in, and for the patients that is very important. People have an idea of what a clinic targeted toward low-income people will look like, and they are surprised when they visit our facility. They say, "Wow, this is as good as any doctor's office or maybe even better." We are proud that we can provide quality space, because we work with a population that greatly relies on us.

The new clinic has allowed us to double the number of patients that we serve. Our prior facility was very restricted in terms of space. It was not built for medical services; it was more of a commercial building, in which all the rooms were partitioned. It is such a huge step forward to have a functional lab. When we were working on the design of the new building, we asked our staff members what they would like to see in the new facility. Their requests were so basic, like having sinks in exam rooms, which we didn't have before. The new clinic has elevated the professionalism and safety of our workers. ▸

the buildings. That's a big deal for nonprofits because they typically live pretty close to the bone. In this case, the McMinnville clinic was used to working in a poor space on a shoestring budget, and this new building opened the organization's eyes to what it could do.

Since our firm was established, our staff has done projects for close to thirty nonprofits. In every one of them, we end up contributing a substantial percentage of our services pro bono. We have always started with the approach that everything that goes around comes around. All of the pro bono work that we've done for our clients has led to long-term relationships and more work. It really hits you on all fronts. It makes us feel good. Our commitment to this work expresses the values of this firm. From a business side, many clients pass our name on to other nonprofit groups and private clients. So we see it as a tremendous market.

Scott | Edwards has come to understand the model of care that we provide and how that model has changed over the years, the differences in where we were ten years ago and where we are today. As we began looking at a new facility in Cornelius, Oregon—which would be our biggest project yet—we brought in Scott | Edwards because the firm already had an intimate knowledge of our operations and how to meet the needs of our thousands of patients. There has not been a project yet too challenging for Scott | Edwards. Every time, the architects roll up their sleeves and work with us to find the best solutions.

YWCA

YWCA Laura Parks and Mildred Francis Center
Location Chicago, Illinois **Date** 2008 **Client** YWCA Metropolitan Chicago **Client liaison** Laura Thrall **Design firm** HOK **Design team** Natalie Banaszak, Tom Polucci, Sheryl Schulze, Susan Skibell **Area** 7,500 sq. ft. **Cost** $516,000 **Estimated value of pro bono design services** $41,000 **Websites** www.ywca.org, www.hok.com

Laura Thrall
Former CEO, YWCA Metropolitan Chicago,
Chicago, Illinois

CLIENT

Our organization began a project, called Model YWCA, that sought to rebrand the entire way we deliver programs and services. Our goal for it was to create a place that embodies the way we want women to feel when they come in to us for services. We wanted a beautiful, welcoming, open space that gives our clients a sense of worth, embraces them, and makes them feel empowered. In the past, our facilities had been old, fairly rundown, and really typical of health and human service agencies that don't have a lot of money. We wanted something bold, edgy, and bright, but that also conveyed a sense of warmth. We wanted people to come in and discover a hip, new YWCA, instead of their grandmothers' YW.

One of the YWCA's dominant service lines is its role as the largest provider of sexual-violence services in the state of Illinois, which means women who are victims of sexual assault often come to our facility for private counseling. Given that, we wanted HOK to understand how we work as an agency, namely, our concerns with confidentiality, the sensitive nature of why the clients come into the space, and the need to treat them with respect.

In the past, the YW centers used to hide themselves in order to protect the anonymity of women seeking sexual-violence counseling, so they were never well branded. This YWCA needed to be more visible to the community. We wanted it to look like a community center—someplace where women can feel comfortable, sit down on the couches, and hang out in the café. It serves as a safe haven, a place where one does not have to feel like a victim. The design evolved around those concepts.

Tom Polucci from HOK really understood all of this. It was clear from the firm's initial designs. We certainly did some tweaking; however, there was not a lot of back-and-forth. Tom and his team learned very quickly about the sensitive work we do, and they expertly translated that into the design features. For example, we did not want the sexual-violence clients to have to enter or exit through the main door, so HOK created a separate waiting area that was more quiet and private and has its own entrance and exit. ▸

Tom Polucci
Director of Interiors, HOK,
Chicago, Illinois

ARCHITECT

Our design process with YWCA was very hands-on; the organization's team was involved from the beginning. This was an important project for them because it was going to be the first of many such centers that they wanted to place throughout the Chicago area. The plan was for this to be a model for the YWCA nationally.

Laura Thrall, the CEO at the time, made all the final decisions, which was great, but she also wanted her staff to be engaged and have ownership and pride in this thing. To accomplish that, we had a "vision session" with literally everyone who was going to work in the space. We sat in a big room and talked about our process, the work, and what they did and did not need. It was really beneficial to understand how they needed the spaces to work. We engaged in conversation and showed lots of pictures of other projects so that we could get a visual understanding of what they were trying to describe. We wanted a common understanding, and doing it this way was helpful.

When this project began, the YWCA had exhaustively rebranded itself to focus more clearly on the women that it served. The central messages of investing in yourself and your children and looking for a better way of life ▸

through counseling or education were apparent throughout the branding materials. As part of this effort, the organization created a series of black-and-white, lovingly photographed portraits of actual clients. There was also a new logo, and persimmon became the official YWCA color. It was very important to Laura that these elements be present throughout the space.

When we were programming the building, the focus became how to create interactive, collaborative, and comfortable environments that would be durable and flexible. We created meeting rooms with sliding panels that open and close to configure a variety of spaces. These panels are framed in maple with polycarbonate on the inside in the signature persimmon color. We created a little café with both high-seating and low-seating meeting spaces. The café also needed to be built like a tank because it is so heavily used. To make the spaces durable, we looked at materials. In the public circulation areas, we sealed the concrete floors instead of polishing them. For the built-in bench chairs, we used hardwoods and laminates, instead of fabrics, so they could be easily cleaned and repaired.

We worked with some great manufacturers that donated materials or gave them at cost. The carpet company Interface and the furniture manufacturer Allsteel were really generous. The general contractor, Skender, worked hard to put ▸

eliminating racism
empowering women
ywca

metropolitan chicago

To emphasize our presence in the community, we wanted the front of the building to be something that established our identity, something more than just a sign. Into the facade, HOK incorporated all of the words that embody our brand—integrity, freedom, power, and justice—as well as images of diverse women from our community. The firm created transparent "wraps" of these elements and covered the four front windows of the building with them. Like an advertisement on a bus window, we can see through the wraps from inside the building, but passersby cannot see inside. They see only the powerful words and images that reflect who we are. The firm also created an eye-popping orange wall in the reception area, which is a great use of a powerful color.

HOK asked all of its preferred vendors to join the cause. The contractor, Skender Construction, gave up its fee and waived its 10 percent over-head. HOK got discounts on carpeting. U.S. Gypsum donated all the wall-board. Tom did a great job of picking durable, nice-looking, inexpensive finishes. HOK also went above and beyond when an issue arose with zoning and permitting. Initially we were told it would take ninety days to resolve an issue with our permit, but HOK was able to get it resolved in two weeks.

This project set a new, fresh tone for the YWCA; it has become the center on which we can model all the others, because it captures what we are all about. Before, in this same neighborhood, we had a decrepit building that was falling apart. The people in the community feel that comparing this new YW to that one is like night and day. They feel that, throughout the space, we've shown how much we value them, and this is extremely important. Just because people lack financial means or live in low-income, underserved communities does not mean they should not feel entitled to high-quality services and beautiful spaces.

everything together for very little money. God bless them: The guys were willing to work with any budget and get the right team out there to build that space. There were a lot of good people doing their absolute best to make this work. It was great to see that kind of effort.

There are many different reasons why I do pro bono projects. I think being part of the community and giving back in some way is important. The work also really enriches our people; they become engaged and involved in a way that makes them so much more committed to HOK and the larger community. Working with a client like the YWCA was very different from working with the typical HOK client. In this case, we have a client who wants our design talent and is willing to say, "Even though you haven't done many projects of this type, I'm really interested in the way you design, and we want to work with you." That's always a good feeling.

We're designers. We love to create spaces. We do a lot of work on interiors, creating office environments and things like that. The opportunity to create a space that is supporting and nurturing for somebody who needs help because she is looking to change her life is incredibly gratifying. It's why most of us became architects or interior designers.

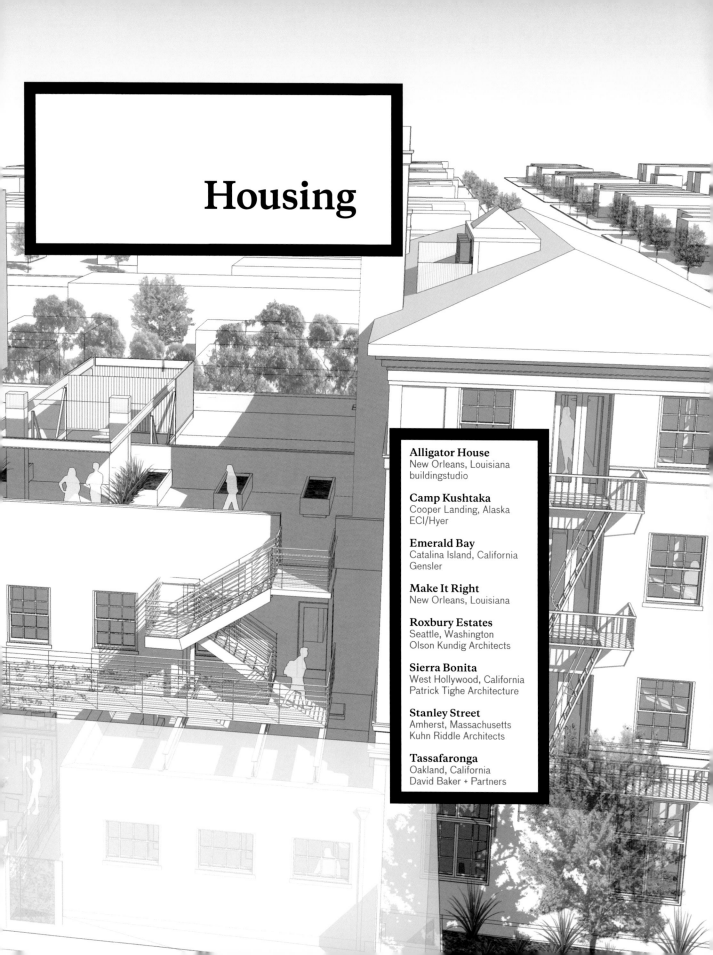

Housing

Alligator House

Alligator House
Location New Orleans, Louisiana **Date** 2009 **Client** Neighborhood Housing Services of New Orleans
Client liaison Randy Michaelson **Design firm** buildingstudio **Design team** Coleman Coker, David
Dieckhoff, Varuni Edussuriya, Tom Holloman, Jonathan Tate **Area** 962 sq. ft. **Cost** $115,000 **Estimated
value of pro bono design services** $50,000 **Websites** www.nhsnola.org, www.buildingstudio.net

Coleman Coker
Principal, buildingstudio,
New Orleans, Louisiana

ARCHITECT

The first year after Hurricane Katrina, my firm worked with Tulane University's URBANbuild program on a house in the Central City neighborhood, just around the block from where the Alligator House is located. The program has now built six houses in that neighborhood, all for NHS. It was a natural progression from having worked through the university to having our office work privately with the group.

At the start of this project, we had a commitment from another client of my firm to help with the cost of the house. We approached NHS and offered to bring some money to the table. They were happy to have us onboard and helped us gauge the leeway for the nontraditional design that we thought was appropriate in a neighborhood of traditional houses.

Architecturally, New Orleans is dominated by single-floor and duplex ▸

Randy Michaelson
Director of Design Build, Neighborhood Housing Services of New Orleans,
New Orleans, Louisiana

CLIENT

Neighborhood Housing Services (NHS) is a one-stop shop for people who are interested in becoming homeowners in New Orleans. We assist new buyers with everything from education about the realities of homeownership to financial planning. We also provide services, such as renovations, repairs, and foreclosure prevention, for existing homeowners. We have been around for thirty-three years, and we have always done some new real estate development to increase the inventory of homes available to low- and moderate-income first-time home buyers. But obviously we now do a lot of work for people returning to New Orleans post-Katrina.

Coleman Coker, our architect on this project, relocated to New Orleans after Hurricane Katrina and became an adjunct professor at the Tulane School of Architecture. A client of Coleman's offered to donate some funds to build a house in New Orleans, so Coleman approached us about teaming up on the project, and off we went.

NHS had an inventory of lots to choose from, but it sounded like a perfect opportunity to tackle a really challenging site. The lot we decided on was less than 19 feet wide and less than 78 feet deep. Lots in New Orleans are notoriously narrow; by comparison, average lots in other regions of the country are 30 feet wide and 90 feet deep. Normally our city's small sites remain undeveloped and become an eyesore or a serious problem for a neighborhood. However, this was a chance to use design to turn a problem property into a property for home ownership. ▸

shotgun homes. Trying to build nontraditional housing in a traditional city, we faced some resistance, but we were building in a neighborhood that had effectively been forgotten by the city. Thus, the residents thought it was positive that someone was doing something so forward thinking on their behalf. We got a lot of receptiveness thanks to that alone.

The residents thought our designs were cool; they related to them. We wanted to show that with some creativity and for essentially the same amount of money that a standard home costs, we could give this neighborhood something special. The folks in Central City, as in many inner-city neighborhoods, feel disenfranchised. They feel that their local government has bypassed their institutions and that they're only going to get the low end of what's available. We wanted to change that in a way that we felt would be uplifting and beneficial to the community. A lot of people complimented us for doing it.

In this house, we developed a strategy to get cross-ventilation at the short axis, and it being a shotgun, the back door also provides good ventilation. We raised the roofline over the main bedroom and the living room to give those rooms high ceilings. In those areas, you can open the windows on both sides in the summer, and with 12-foot ceilings and fans, you really don't need air conditioning. The envelope was very important to us; we used ▹

The house needed to have at least two bedrooms and two bathrooms. In terms of area, it had to be between 900 and 1,000 square feet. Our standard requirement when building a home is to have three bedrooms and two baths, totaling approximately 1,200 square feet, but we made an exception given the circumstances and the size of the lot. Usually we are dealing with a single parent or a family with more than one child, so we feel there must be more than two bedrooms. Coleman made a number of space-saving decisions in the house, including the installation of an operable wall system in lieu of a standard door, which provided some flexibility. The resulting space could be used as a bedroom or office.

I think some of the greatest design elements of the house are where the roof slopes up in the rear, above the master bedroom, and where it slopes up in the front, above the kitchen and living area. The side profile and the front facade remind people of an alligator, which is where the house's name comes from. The slopes create an impression of spaciousness in two very important rooms. We always consider the master bedroom to be important because people like to have some closets and room for furnishings. The vaulted ceilings create a feeling of space that houses of this square footage often do not have.

We consider the Alligator House a great success. Everyone who goes inside loves the floor plan and the space. The modern design of the exterior takes some time to get used to, but we have been doing some other modern housing developments in the surrounding community. This house, in fact, is at the same intersection as a few of the homes built through our partnership with Tulane University's URBANbuild program, which gives students the opportunity to design and construct homes in the city.

2-by-6-foot exterior walls with heavy insulation and insulated glass windows, things that you would use on a typical house but never on a low-cost house. We tried to be as sustainable as possible to keep costs down.

There was a lot of expectation in New Orleans after Hurricane Katrina that architects and designers should do more pro bono work. There's still an attitude that if so many people are offering support, why aren't architects doing more, particularly in affordable housing. The people who work in our office are addressing that. We're not getting paid a lot on these projects, but the work is rewarding as a community service, as something outside of what a typical architecture studio would take on. There really is an opportunity for building affordable, well-designed homes here, if a group of designers is willing to go the extra mile.

Camp Kushtaka

Camp Kushtaka Cabins
Location Cooper Landing, Alaska **Date** 2009 **Client** Camp Fire USA Alaska Council **Client liaison** Barbara Dubovich **Design firm** ECI/Hyer **Design team** Sean Carlson, Margaret Friar, Katie Haese, Brian Meissner, Jae Shin **Area** 3,160 sq. ft. **Cost** $750,000 **Estimated value of pro bono design services** $80,000 **Websites** www.ecihyer.com; www.campfireak.org

Brian Meissner
Principal, ECI/Hyer,
Anchorage, Alaska

ARCHITECT

Steve Fishback, a former principal of our firm, went to one of Camp Fire's fund-raising breakfasts, made a gift, and fell in love in with the program. Eventually he served on the board and did the project management for these cabins. I also fell in love with the camp when I got involved. Originally our team wanted to help update the organization's master plan, and that project grew over the years to include the cabins. Hopefully, we will keep working there until the whole camp has been updated.

Right now, the camp accommodates sixty-four kids, and the aim is to grow capacity to ninety-six. The plan also involves replacing the dining hall, which is the social heart of the camp, and creating an arts facility, storage for boats, caretaker facilities, a cabin for staff, and a health facility.

Before, the camp had many little cabins distributed through the woods and along the shoreline of Kenai Lake, on land ▸

Barbara Dubovich
CEO, Camp Fire USA Alaska Council,
Anchorage, Alaska

CLIENT

Kenai Lake, where Camp Kushtaka is located, is a phenomenal site. It is one of the most majestic places in Alaska, and for many of our youths, being there is their first experience in the outdoors. I know most people think of Alaska as all wilderness, but we also have urban communities. Some children coming out of Anchorage are getting to experience the lakes, trees, squirrels, and mountains for the first time. There is a rustic quality to the experience we provide, and ECI/Hyer was able to capture the spirit of an old camp in its design.

Our old cabins dated back to the 1960s. They were actually second-hand U.S. Forest Service cabins that were taken down at other sites and rebuilt at our camp. They were put together by very dedicated, passionate volunteers who may or may not have had any carpentry skills. The cabins had a tremendously long life, but they were far past their expiration dates. For the future, we wanted facilities that were low cost to maintain and would have a very long life for the organization.

During our camp planning process, we had worked with a firm based in another state, but we then went to ECI/Hyer because we wanted a master plan that felt more Alaskan. During the process, the architects also assisted us with other pro bono design work, including helping us move our main office to a warehouse space in Anchorage. When it came time to work on Camp Kushtaka, we had a diverse building committee, and we were pretty informed as an agency about the steps that needed to be taken. ECI/Hyer sat down with all of us and talked through our priorities, needs, and vision. The architects also spent time at the camp. They watched the comings and goings of the kids and the kinds of activities they're involved in. The firm also talked to our staff and to people in the community about the needs of the camp. The team spent a considerable amount of time gathering as much information as possible from all stakeholders. ▸

leased from the Alaska Department of Natural Resources. The two settings were great for the campers' experience, but they were very challenging from the standpoints of managing the kids and protecting the lake. The project became a matter of consolidating the camps. As part of the deal to renew the camp's lease with the Department of Natural Resources, we had to show that we could move the camp up away from the lake, consolidate it, and not disrupt the wildlife and woods.

The new cabins are really simple—they look like they were built by hand because they were. They were originally designed with the idea that volunteers would do some of the construction, so they couldn't have many components. To avoid damaging the ground, we drove steel pilings into the frozen earth. On top of the pilings, we built a structural platform to support the wood-frame shed construction. It's a little didactic, but it's pretty cool.

Another really simple move was to slope the roofs of the cabins in line with the hill. The typical approach, especially for Americans on a lake, is to tip it the other way. This simple feature minimized the view of the cabins from the lake.

As a master plan, the camp is basically off the grid—it's an old-school, low-tech approach with new innovations. We hope to implement a system for hydroelectric power supported by photovoltaic cells. ▸

What we really appreciate is that the cabins have a very practical design. They have long-term sustainability in mind, which is great from my perspective when I think about the future of the organization twenty, thirty, or even fifty years out. I see the structures enduring that long, but when children come here, they are still camping overnight, staying in cabins with sleeping bags and bunks. By listening to alumni and current staff, ECI/Hyer caught the essence of that experience. The architects were able to deliver the sustainable buildings while maintaining the feeling of being in the outdoors.

The firm took our idea of a campfire, a place where children come together, and changed the design of the cabins' decks to create that idea of a gathering space. The decks are staged, so each has the best views of the property and is large enough to create a nice communal area out of doors. They are also covered so we can work with children in the outdoors during inclement weather. I was impressed with how the firm listened so carefully and translated that into the design.

What was most impressive, however, was that everyone engaged in the process became personally involved. People still bring their spouses and families to volunteer. They chop wood and haul supplies. They know our leadership staff by first name, and we know their kids' names. They've become part of the Camp Fire family, which has formed a very strong working relationship.

I think the architects saw the value of the work, but they also made it fun. Any other architecture firm would say, "We'll do the design work for you." That would have been a tremendous gift, but ECI/Hyer's value is that they have taken it so much further. They were the first firm to come forward and offer pro bono work for our agency. PDC Engineers followed, and together the firms did the architectural design and engineering all pro bono. That resonates with people. ECI/Hyer is known for follow-through, and the firm brought eighteen other companies to the table offering pro bono services to help build the cabins. In addition to PDC, these included Alcan Electrical & Engineering, Davis Construction & Engineers, Neeser Construction, Partusch Plumbing & Heating, and Universal Roofing of Alaska. That is remarkable.

We would use the solar power, when it's available, to pump well water into the reservoir at the top of the hill. A pipe would bring that water down to camp, and we would use the kinetic energy of the water to generate electricity for cooking. The water treatment process would be more complete, and we wouldn't dump nitrates into the lake.

The camp project has been a long process and a lot of fun. Twice a year, Camp Kushtaka has a big volunteer event, and we've sent teams down almost every time in the last eight years. We've helped stabilize an existing cabin, built a yurt, and installed handrails for them. We also went down while camp was in session. We get to talk to staff, and we've had a lot of interaction just as volunteers ourselves.

The contractors we engaged to work on the cabins are two of the biggest in Alaska: Davis and Nesser. At the beginning, we had a commitment from the engineering firm to donate its services, and from there it snowballed to these big contractors and even their subcontractors donating services. The carpenters loved this project. For the most part, the people were the absolute best from each company, including the superintendents and project managers—the ones who don't get a chance to wear tool belts much anymore. We sucked them in, and the next thing we knew, everyone was saying they'd make something work. It was totally unexpected. ▶

I think when people find out what we did for Camp Fire and that we aren't out trumpeting it, they understand our firm culture much better. We moved the project around and let everyone in the office have time with it. That's important to us. It's not just the inexperienced people or the people who are available. It helps us develop our firm's values. At one of the Camp Fire board meetings they asked me, "Why do you do it?" I told them we are kind of addicted to Camp Fire—the joy we get from the work, and the joy we get from seeing the camp.

Emerald Bay

Camp Emerald Bay Eco Cabins
Location Catalina Island, California **Date** 2009 **Client** Boy Scouts of America Western Los Angeles County Council **Client liaison** Lee Harrison **Design firm** Gensler **Design team** Peter Barsuk, Richard Hammond, Robert Jernigan **Area** Six cabins, each 320 sq. ft. **Cost** $300,000 **Estimated value of pro bono design services** $20,000 **Websites** www.bsa.org, www.gensler.com

Robert Jernigan and
Richard Hammond
Principal and Project
Architect, Gensler,
Los Angeles, California

ARCHITECT

Gensler's Los Angeles office has a long-standing relationship with the Boy Scouts of America and Camp Emerald Bay on Catalina Island, and some of our employees' sons are scouts. One of the main objectives of the camp is to teach kids leadership and ethics. Part of being on an island is that everything has to be transported over and back, so the notion of sustainability is critical.

When we began thinking about a new cabin design for the camp, we knew we didn't want the kids to leave Los Angeles and go and stay in another building similar to their homes; we wanted something different. In our design conversations, we kept talking about transformation. We want to see these young people learn to appreciate the environment and, hopefully, come back changed individually.

We wanted a sustainable building, and we ultimately decided to use ▶

Lee Harrison
Executive Director, Camp Emerald Bay,
Catalina Island, California

CLIENT

Camp Emerald Bay was founded in 1925, and it has been run continuously by the Boy Scouts of America, except for a brief period during World War II when it was turned into a military base. The camp is a recurring, one-week program for scouts that develops outdoor skills, leadership, and ethical conduct. In the last fifteen years, we've expanded our programs and the camp's usage, and we are actually open about nine months of the year. In the spring and fall, school programs come during the week, and on weekends, we rent out the camp to YMCAs, Sierra Clubs, and other Boy and Girl Scout groups. We see about 14,000 campers every year.

Statistically, there are two things that kids from economically disadvantaged environments commonly don't experience: One is horses, and the other is the ocean. Being able to bring kids who don't have that exposure to experience some of the educational tools here—the marine science program or just the ocean itself—is a great opportunity. We try to bring in local kids from the Long Beach and Los Angeles areas of California and give them an experience that they probably couldn't get any other way.

We have a long-term relationship with Gensler that dates back ten to fifteen years. The firm helped us develop our master plan in 1998, and Rob Jernigan, who has a young child in scouting, reconnected with us when we wanted to implement some new projects related to ecology and conservation. One of the biggest things about scouting is working to leave the smallest environmental footprint you can. Because the ecological challenges on the island become more and more apparent each year, we looked at how we could create some structures at the camp that articulate our "leave no trace" mission. Since the 1960s, the cabins used at Camp Emerald Bay were unique A-frame structures that had been made from an aluminum material used by the region's aviation industry.

We came up with the idea of using shipping containers to replace those aging cabins as we thought about our location and our connection to ▶

shipping containers, which are probably the biggest reusable containers you can find. There's a surplus of used containers out there, and our contractor actually donated them free of charge. Containers are structurally rigid, so each cabin could be held up on a few points and touch the ground in only a few spots, which helped keep the ecological footprint small.

Shipping container architecture is not exactly new, but we wanted to create a pleasant environment, so we removed the container tops and added translucent fabric roofs. This design was inspired by Frank Lloyd Wright's Taliesin West, which has canvas roofs. Taliesin is in a desert environment, which is harsher than Catalina's, and the canvas roofs have served those buildings well for over sixty years.

Boats and sails also inspired the design for the roofs. We started with that idea because there's an obvious connection between the island and that type of structural system. We didn't want to have a traditional pitched roof like the other buildings out there, which use a lot of wood and shingles and create waste. These are lightweight structures built with minimal materials, and we actually shipped them out in the containers they now cover. The long rigid beams are just the right length to fit in the container.

The translucent fabric roofs are 8 feet high on the sides and go up to about 13.5 feet in the center. What everybody ▶

Los Angeles, one of the largest ports in the world. When we introduced the idea to our staff, people's heads cocked to the side a bit; their vision of a shipping container is an ugly steel structure. Generally, the containers are either covered with graffiti or dented. The staff's attitude was, "Okay, I don't really understand it yet, but we're willing to take on the task of looking at it as a possibility."

Not only are we in Los Angeles County, which has tough permitting laws, but we're also on a privately owned island, so there were a lot of challenges. The county doesn't allow sea containers on the island, so the local government immediately questioned our use of them. I kept saying, "It's not a sea container; it's a construction material." It took us over a year to get the permit. It was a very difficult and delicate process, navigating through all the different agencies.

With costs in mind, we tried to look at not just the physical structure of the facility but also how we use our resources. One of the things Gensler has helped us do is to keep thinking beyond our normal practices, so that we become more effective educators. We want to have a cohesive narrative for fund-raising and marketing purposes and to be able to use our facilities as talking points. The Eco Cabins are great teaching tools for us, tying in concepts of sustainability and connecting them with what is happening in the camp.

Regardless of what his economic background is, when you take a boy out of his normal social environment, you get to see him blossom. Giving somebody an opportunity to have a different experience— even if that means just going ten blocks from his home—often exposes him to something he would never know about himself or about other people. That's why we love Camp Emerald Bay so much. It has a natural tendency to do that for people—they come out here and experience all this growth. You get to see people do things they never would have done otherwise.

seems to like so much when they walk into the Eco Cabins is how spacious they are. We can fit eight kids in one cabin. The cabins are light and airy, so you can sit inside and read in the daytime. In front of each cabin, there is a 6-foot deck, which is made of wood from an old pier that was recently replaced.

We cannot underplay Lee Harrison's guts in going with us on some of these ideas, and his foresight in convincing the local fire chief and the island's conservancy to test some of their preconceived notions about using containers. This project was truly a testament to his fortitude. You have to have a willing, accepting client, and Lee was both. In addition, he is a great orchestrator; he got many of the scout fathers involved in construction. The terrific thing about the camp is that everyone wants to do something, to give something.

On all of our pro bono projects, we put together what we think is a reasonable projection of costs and then try to run it like any other job, even though there is no money coming in. The firm pays us for some of our time but not all of it. We have spent a lot of weekends going to the island and overseeing the construction of the Eco Cabins on our own time. It is really important that we as employees make commitments.

Pro bono projects touch and change people's lives. Our hope is that twenty or thirty years from now, one of us will run into ▸

some young man who will say, "I went to this camp and learned about the environment and stayed in this cabin, and it made me a different person." That's what we hope, and we can almost promise you it will happen. Someone will say that to us one of these days, and I think that's what it's all about. In giving, you really do receive.

Make It Right

Make It Right Homes
Location New Orleans, Louisiana **Date** 2008–present **Client** Make It Right Foundation **Client liaison** Tom Darden **Design team** 21 architecture firms; GRAFT, design advisor; William McDonough + Partners, sustainability advisor; John C. Williams Architects, executive architect **Estimated value of pro bono design services** Not available **Websites** www.makeitrightnola.org, www.graftlab.com, www.mcdonoughpartners.com, www.williamsarchitects.com

Adjaye Associates
London, United Kingdom
Single-family home

Atelier Hitoshi Abe
Sendai, Japan
Duplex home

Bild Design
New Orleans, Louisiana
Duplex home

Billes Architecture
New Orleans, Louisiana
Single-family home

BNIM
Houston, Texas
Single-family home, duplex home

buildingstudio
New Orleans, Louisiana
Duplex home

Concordia
New Orleans, Louisiana
Single-family home

Constructs
Accra, Ghana
Single-family home, duplex home

ELEMENTAL
Santiago, Chile
Duplex home

Eskew+Dumez+Ripple
New Orleans, Louisiana
Single-family home

Gehry Partners
Los Angeles, California
Duplex home

GRAFT
Berlin, Germany
Single-family home, duplex home

Kappe Architects/Planners
Los Angeles, California
Duplex home

KieranTimberlake Associates
Philadelphia, Pennsylvania
Single-family home

Morphosis
Santa Monica, California
Single-family home

MVRDV
Rotterdam, The Netherlands
Single-family home, duplex home

Pugh + Scarpa Architects
Santa Monica, California
Single-family home, duplex home

Shigeru Ban Architects
Tokyo, Japan
Single-family home

Trahan Architects
Baton Rouge, Louisiana
Single-family home

Waggonner & Ball Architects
New Orleans, Louisiana
Duplex home

William McDonough + Partners
Charlottesville, Virginia
Duplex home

Tom Darden
Executive Director, Make It Right Foundation,
New Orleans, Louisiana

William McDonough
and Jose Atienza
Principal and Senior
Designer, William
McDonough + Partners,
Charlottesville, Virginia

CLIENT

On August 29, 2005, Hurricane Katrina ripped through New Orleans and devastated the Gulf Coast of the United States. Our founder, Brad Pitt, saw what happened with the storm and wanted to help. He had filmed some movies down here and fell in love with the city and the people. He had also participated as a sponsor of the Global Green design competition, which was planning to build five single-family homes, one multifamily unit, and a community center soon after the storm. Brad wanted to do more and wondered if we could take that concept and roll it out on a larger scale, bringing families back to the Lower Ninth Ward and giving them homes. Around that time, he had read architect Bill McDonough's book, *Cradle to Cradle*, which outlines principles and guidelines for environmentally safe and socially responsible building. Brad called Bill and said, "I read your book. I want to do more to help New Orleans, and I want anything that we build to be based on the principles of *Cradle to Cradle*." That was in December 2006, the same month that Make It Right was founded.

Bill's firm, William McDonough + Partners, committed on a pro bono basis to oversee Make It Right's work from a sustainability perspective. The firm worked, and continues to work, with the other architects to help them understand the philosophy of *Cradle to Cradle* and how that translates to design, including basic things, like passive heating and cooling strategies. Bill's firm has taken on the responsibility of evaluating and overseeing all of the products used for the houses to make sure they meet the guidelines.

The architecture firm GRAFT was another key partner from early on. It was with GRAFT that Brad came up with the idea of inviting architects from all over the world—as well as multiple firms in New Orleans—to be part of Make It Right and actually do the design work. With GRAFT, we started to reach out to firms, and today we have twenty-one firms participating, thirteen of which have been with us from the beginning. We give each one a set of design guidelines, including basic parameters for the size of the house, and extensive research on the city's housing and architecture for reference. ▶

ARCHITECT

We believe that to make quality buildings, you need quality materials. Our office is deeply focused on that. When Hurricane Katrina hit, we wanted to do something to help, but we were not sure how to make ourselves available. Then Brad Pitt called and asked us to get involved. We started to imagine what we might be able to do, and together we imagined Make It Right. The way we thought about this wasn't, "Let's build and sell houses." It was, "Let's help people coming home." But in reality that was incredibly complex: We had to figure out who owned all the empty lots in the Ninth Ward and who had titles. It involved a large amount of assessments, paperwork, and identification. We had to facilitate the process of getting people home on a practical level.

The mission of Make It Right includes using principles put forth in *Cradle to Cradle*. To help instill those, our firm elected to stay back from designing one *thing*, like a house, at least during the first round. We wanted to focus instead on helping all the designers work with material assessments and performance standards to get to a higher level of design and building. We developed a protocol on material selection, energy, and water, and we shared that information with ▶

all the teams. We have produced documents explaining these concepts, and we also put a member of our staff on this project full-time, pro bono, to be available to the teams, answer questions, and provide information.

It was wonderful to work with the other architects. These people are busy. They are all over the world designing megaprojects, but they come down to New Orleans to build these small houses. When we have been with them, we see their commitment and interest in creating a community and building healthy homes for these people. That makes this project work.

In terms of gaining the residents' trust, it was a matter of being forthright and honest and showing people that we were offering something with true value. In the beginning, we were very focused on just trying to get some houses there. People had been displaced for a long time; there was an urgent need for housing and simply to get people back in the neighborhood. Our initial goal for Make It Right was to build 150 houses, and we are currently on target for that.

At the same time that we are building homes, we are also looking at what community facilities we can create. We are wide open to providing as many amenities as possible, within the scope of our resources and the interests of the community. For example, our firm developed a protocol around streetscapes and how the streets can be developed in new ways ▶

page 229
Billes Architecture

above
Lower Ninth Ward, New Orleans, post-Katrina

opposite top and bottom
William McDonough + Partners
Flow House. Renderings

with porous paving. Some of that paving has already been implemented for sidewalks in the neighborhood.

After the first single-family homes were built, there was a request from the community for duplex homes. Some of the residents were saying, "It would be wonderful if I had a small rental," or, "My ideal would be if I could take in more of my extended family to live with us." Once we heard that, we had more workshops about what the duplex homes could be and what the community wanted from them. Some of the people already placed by Make It Right came to those sessions and talked with people who didn't yet have houses. It was amazing to hear the people who had moved in educate the others about the structures' sustainable features and how great they are. They explained how the solar panels work and how the solar thermal works. It was wonderful watching them get so enthusiastic about it.

During this duplex design stage, our firm decided to design a home because we thought we could incorporate a lot of what we had learned into one structure. We designed Flow House to be flexible so we could experiment with many different building methods to see which is the most cost-effective. Shade was a huge consideration. We also thought about design for disassembly, so that if someday this house were to be removed, the materials would be identifiable and could be reused. We looked at air ▸

distribution to provide excellent cross-ventilation, which is very important in New Orleans. This house is very modest; the budgets were tight, obviously, so we tried to keep it affordable, practical, and adaptable.

Part of what Make It Right is doing is creating a type of laboratory. The organization builds many types of houses and improves on the prototypes as the teams continue to build more. When they build a house, they might use a particular building method, and perhaps the next time, they might adapt and use something else. The first building might be a spec-built house, the next a modular system, and the following panelized construction. Through experimentation, Make It Right finds the most cost-effective way to build each home in terms of time and materials. The process, thus far, has been very successful.

Flow House is an adaptable building that can be reconfigured over time. You can extend the first floor and make it larger. For us, the most successful aspect of the home is this flexibility—it allows families to grow and change. It also allows them to be connected to the exterior. We felt it was important to create an outdoor space for gatherings and celebrations, so we tried to design the footprint of the house to have the least impact on the property and landscape as possible. You can have a duplex home but also have ample outdoor space to grow vegetables and be outside. ▶

To give you a sense of what makes our work with the Make It Right Foundation so important to me, one of the most meaningful moments recently occurred in New York at the Clinton Global Initiative, where Bill Clinton, Brad Pitt, and I [Bill McDonough] were on stage with a resident of a Make It Right home. In the middle of the panel, this resident stood up and said, "My family had been away from home for three years, and we had been living in a trailer in another state. We are now home in our city, and we are living in a home we can afford. My kids each have a room. Our house was beautifully built by an international architect, and my energy bill is $24 each month, which means my daughter can take ballet lessons." And then she said something amazing. "Understand one other thing: My daughter has asthma, and I spent years waking up to the sound of her coughing. Do you know what that is like? When we moved into the new house, her asthma went away." The daughter can take ballet lessons and breathe. We are talking about quality of life here.

We made clear to each participating firm that the only way we were going to build the house it designed was if the plan was selected by one of the families that we were helping. That was important for the firms to know at the outset, because we wanted to encourage them to participate in the design process with the community. We conducted design charrettes, which were the primary up front interactions between the design architects and the families. From there, the families selected one of the designs that we had available and then worked with our executive architect, John C. Williams Architects, a firm here in New Orleans, to engage in any modifications to that plan.

Right now, we have thirteen single-family home designs and fourteen duplex designs. Twelve of the single-family designs have been selected, which is pretty amazing to me. The diversity of opinions that these families have on the designs is so interesting. Every family that we work with thinks that theirs is the best house, which is the best part as far as I'm concerned. Our goal, since Make It Right was founded, is to build at least 150 homes.

Sometimes the families who wind up in these homes find us, but more often, we seek them out. We have people on our staff dedicated to that task, and it is an amazing challenge given how displaced the community is. Once we find them, the process varies depending on if the family owns a piece of property on which we can build or if they will move into a property that Make It Right has acquired.

The response from the families that have moved in has been 100 percent positive, and that, too, is really exciting. They appreciate the functionality of the designs. For some, it's the lighting that a particular design affords or the shading or the front porch. All the houses and the different variations of colors are selections that were made by the families, and many of them love having that choice. It's a little risky from a neighborhood planning perspective, but it's been fun to see the neighborhood take shape in the colors that these families choose.

The improvements to the families' day-to-day lives are amazing. We don't have a ton of data yet, but anecdotal evidence is showing us that the residents are healthier now than when they lived elsewhere, particularly regarding respiratory conditions. Energy bills for our houses are very low; on average they are $35 per month, compared to about $250 in my own house in New Orleans, for example. The families really appreciate that. And they think it's cool to be part of this innovative project in this innovative neighborhood. There's even a homeowners group for Make It Right families that has come together and now meets every two weeks. It's a way that they can approach our organization if there's something communal they want to discuss like street lighting, where contractors park their trucks, or traffic (over forty tour buses go through the neighborhood each day), as opposed to coming to us individually. That makes things more efficient on our end, but the more important aspect of it is that the residents self-organized the group.

All of the families who are back in this neighborhood truly want to be here. In many respects, they're pioneers. There were only four families, living in FEMA trailers, in the northern section of the neighborhood immediately after the storm. The area in which we're building the Make It Right homes was previously right in front of the levee, so the houses were just washed away. There wasn't even any power to some of the FEMA trailers when I was first working with those families. Now to be living in such a cool neighborhood is really meaningful and a point of pride for these people. ▷

pages 232–33
clockwise from top left
Billes Architecture;
Eskew+Dumez+Ripple;
Morphosis, Float House;
Concordia;
Trahan Architects;
Billes Architecture;
Eskew+Dumez+Ripple;
Shigeru Ban Architects

opposite top
KieranTimberlake Associates

opposite bottom
Melba Leggett in her home
designed by KieranTimberlake
Associates

The U.S. Green Building Council is officially calling this the largest collection of green affordable houses that are LEED Platinum certified anywhere in the country. In some ways, that's sad: It's such a small number. But we'll continue to grow, which is part of the reason I think the council feels comfortable saying that. We also had the fastest construction of a LEED Platinum house, and we built the first modular LEED Platinum home. There are some achievements that we can readily and tangibly point to, but building any house for a family in the Lower Ninth Ward is a huge achievement. We're proud of our ability to do that and the chance to work with these families. It's an extreme situation in every way, from the initial devastation to creating a design strategy that accommodates the risk associated with future storms and flooding. I think we've made some real progress in that regard. For example, in its design for Make It Right, the firm Morphosis developed the first floating foundation that's been permitted in the U.S. It has great potential as a model for homes in other low-lying areas.

Thanks to the way this program has been developed, we're able to tap into amazing design expertise on a pro bono basis, and that allows us to do a lot more than for-profit developers can when they have to pay these experts. This system allows us to push the envelope and really innovate, while creating the best possible homes and circumstances for families returning to New Orleans and the Lower Ninth Ward.

Roxbury Estates

Roxbury Estates
Location Seattle, Washington **Date** 2003 **Client** Habitat for Humanity of Seattle/South King County **Client liaison** Diane Gallegos **Design firm** Olson Kundig Architects **Design team** Kristen Becker, Brad Conway, Andrew Enright, Olivier Landa, Rick Sundberg, Matthias Winkler, Stephen Wood, Stephen Yamada-Heidner, Suzanne Zahr **Area** Site, 38,800 sq. ft.; average individual house, 1,200 sq. ft. **Estimated value of pro bono design services** $150,000 **Websites** www.seattle-habitat.org, www.olsonkundigarchitects.com

Diane Gallegos
COO, Habitat for Humanity of Seattle/South King County,
Seattle, Washington

CLIENT

Habitat for Humanity in Seattle had engaged architects in the past but never to the extent that we involved Olson Kundig Architects on the Roxbury Estates project. We needed a firm that would be open minded and receptive to community input. Though there had been some crime issues in the neighborhood, there was a very active group of residents working hard to take its community back.

Roxbury Estates was an incredibly exciting, challenging project. There was a large undeveloped property in the community that was owned by the Episcopal diocese. Habitat for Humanity had never worked on an undeveloped site in that area before. We wanted to build a community of ten homes. We had to accommodate families of different sizes with very different cultural backgrounds, so it was necessary to have small and large homes and to keep them affordable. The houses contain between two and five bedrooms. We also built both single-story and two-story homes, which was not common for us. We had done some duplexes before but never this kind of a mix on one site.

We were really interested in making the buildings as durable and sustainable as possible. Olson Kundig also worked very hard with us to make the homes affordable. Because of the design and construction of the houses, the long-term maintenance and utilities costs are low.

The architects really listened to us. There was a lot of give and take, back and forth. We closely evaluated products, colors, and other elements. The surrounding homes in the community are dominated by pastels, and we came in with a more modern design and vibrant colors. It's a very diverse community that includes families born here in the U.S. and immigrant families, but they all loved the colors. We pushed the envelope in many ways, and this took some courage on everyone's part, including our donors. A number of community groups sponsored the homes, and doing ten homes at one time was an opportunity for us to really grow the capacity of our organization. ▶

Rick Sundberg
Principal, Olson Kundig Architects,
Seattle, Washington

ARCHITECT

Some of our employees—including myself and many of the younger members of the firm—had volunteered from time to time on Saturday construction projects for Habitat for Humanity. Our firm had also done small pro bono projects here and there but nothing of quite this scale. When Habitat for Humanity approached us with this project for ten houses, we agreed after very little discussion, and I became the principal for it. We hadn't done any low-cost housing in the past, and we were really intrigued. We're kind of a high-end firm, so this was exercising a lot of muscles that I hadn't used in many years.

Our scheme started with the *parti* for the site plan, which had already been developed. We wanted the houses to have entries off of the public street as well as from the semipublic space in the back of the houses. But we felt very strongly that we didn't want to turn the project completely in on itself. We wanted the houses to have front doors and porches on the street, more or less like what you might find elsewhere in that neighborhood. ▶

In the Northwest, 78 percent of our days are overcast, so lighting is a huge consideration. We decided to take something simple—the window—and personalize it. By placing windows in different locations that are a little outside the norm, we were able to play with how light sneaks into a room. We also incorporated color on the exterior of the homes to give each some identity. Each door is also a bit personalized. It was a very simple design strategy to make the place more enjoyable. With the climate of the Northwest, you need color.

We wanted to use different kinds of exterior skins on the houses. We actually designed them with all sorts of corrugated concrete panels, but the shipping on those was really expensive. Instead we went back to work with plain, flat panels of Hardie board and batting to get the texture that we were looking for. The enlarged battens cast a little bit more shadow, which became an inexpensive but effective way to give more life to something that would have been flat otherwise.

For me, from an intellectual and planning point of view, the most interesting piece of the project was the site plan. But, quite frankly, it looked really good on paper and wasn't nearly as successful in real life as I hoped it would be, partially because everyone ran out of money, time, and energy for the landscaping. We had an intense idea of flow from parking lot to common public space to semiprivate spaces in ▶

239

the yards of the inhabitants. It was pretty dependent on landscaping, and it failed. This was an instructive lesson, because we designed too complex a landscape for folks who may be working two jobs and raising children and don't have time in the evenings to clip plants or weed garden beds. We'd given them areas for vegetable gardens that they simply didn't have the time for. It kind of broke my heart. We really needed to do a much simpler scheme.

Before designing their homes, I also should have gotten to know some of the families better to learn how they lived. For instance, I went to visit one of the families afterward, and I realized that with a few little nuances in design, I could have made the house a much more positive space for them. They love the house, but it could have been better without costing more money. That got me thinking that next time I do this kind of work, I need to have a lot more information about the folks who will be using the homes.

I now spend 50 percent of my time on projects like this. Whether I work across the street, across the country, or on the other side of the world, it really doesn't make much difference. I find it's not about altruism; it's simply about trying to solve a problem that needs to be solved.

I think the livability of the houses is the most successful aspect of the project. The design serves the families, and the families love their homes. The houses are small, but because of window placement and that sort of thing, when you walk into them, they feel very open and much bigger than they really are. When you walk in, you say, "Wow, this is a beautiful home." It doesn't look like stereotypical low-income housing.

Olson Kundig designed the site so that the front yards are smaller, and the activity and play spaces in back are more communal. For the residents, living close together and with shared space resulted in some struggles. However, in navigating those disagreements, we worked closely with the families and were able to design features to help them develop the community that they wanted.

Almost five years after the project was completed, Rick Sundberg came and spent an entire day with the community, going through a charrette about the common areas because the families were having some problems maintaining those spaces. It meant a great deal to the residents and to our organization that the architect made that kind of long-term investment in the success of the project.

The neighborhood has reacted well to the design. Our homes have been featured in annual community garden tours. The pride the homeowners have in these beautiful homes is incredible. One family has moved on, but the rest are there, and I don't think any of them are leaving anytime soon. The expectation is that their children will one day have families in those homes.

Sierra Bonita

Sierra Bonita Affordable Housing
Location West Hollywood, California **Date** 2010 **Client** West Hollywood Community Housing Corporation
Client liaison Robin Conerly, executive director **Design firm** Patrick Tighe Architecture **Design team**
Nick Hopson, Yosuke Hoshina, Lisa Little, Karla Mueller, Jarod Poenisch, Peter Storey, Patrick Tighe, Risa
Tsutsumi **Area** 37,000 sq. ft. **Cost** $12.5 million **Estimated value of pro bono design services** $100,000
Websites www.whchc.org, www.tighearchitecture.com

Ric Abramson
Former Vice-Chair, West Hollywood Community Housing Corporation,
West Hollywood, California

CLIENT

When the Sierra Bonita Affordable Housing project began, I was the vice chair of the board of directors and a member of the design and development committee for the West Hollywood Community Housing Corporation. We were interested in engaging new architectural talent, and the design and development committee really pushed for that as well. We wanted to take a fresh look at affordable housing, as opposed to going with a firm that had done it many times in the past. We identified three or four tentative choices in Southern California, approaching and interviewing each of them, and Patrick Tighe Architecture was among that group.

I had been familiar with Patrick Tighe's work for years and was really interested in his design perspective. West Hollywood is a very creative city, so it seemed like a good match. We were confident he could meet our needs for the project and bring real innovation.

Since I am an architect, I worked with Patrick and helped usher the project through the city approval process. We worked as a team, including holding community meetings with different constituencies in the city. The building is located in the city's redevelopment zone, which has a separate municipal committee comprised of a group of business owners and residents. We presented the project to them, along with other groups, but there was no great outcry about any aspect of our plan.

When we do an affordable housing project, it is usually targeted toward a specific population, whether families or low-income individuals. In this case, we wanted the building to serve seniors and people with special needs. We on the design committee felt very strongly that when you have a population that is less physically able, the connection to the outside world becomes much more important. So we asked Patrick to explore an internal courtyard with cross-ventilated units that had natural lighting during the day and the potential for scenic views. This way, our residents who are homebound or less mobile would still be connected to the city in some way, whether via the internal garden or the windows onto the street. ▷

Patrick Tighe
Principal, Patrick Tighe
Architecture,
Santa Monica, California

ARCHITECT

A few years ago, Paul Zimmerman, the former executive director of the West Hollywood Community Housing Corporation, asked our firm to present a scheme for a site that the organization had acquired along with the city of West Hollywood. The mandate was to create a dense, mixed-use building for a corner lot along one of Los Angeles's busiest thoroughfares, Santa Monica Boulevard. Along with the living units, the project required retail space, as much on-site parking as possible, common space, and the necessary outdoor areas. Our scheme provided forty-two apartments, along with 4,000 square feet of retail at grade and two levels of subterranean parking.

We addressed the density issue by stacking relatively small, efficient units. The apartments are all one-bedroom, 620 square feet with 8-foot ceilings. Although they are compact, an open plan and a relatively simple material palette combine to make them feel larger. We designated the exterior wall in each apartment as a window wall to let in the maximum amount of light. The materials used, such as the exposed concrete floors, were chosen for their durability and environmental impact.

A few years ago, the city of West Hollywood asked us for input on its initiative to draft criteria for green buildings in the ▷

community. This building serves as a pilot for its newly implemented green building ordinance. Photovoltaic arrays provide power, as well as shading for the two fifth-floor terraces. Another system of solar panels is located on the roof and is used to heat the water for the building. The courtyard garden creates a microclimate and offers cross-ventilation through each of the units, lessening the need for cooling devices. We also installed custom exterior screens on all window walls for sun protection and privacy.

The building is of steel construction; a series of moment frames was used to allow for maximum windows, and a braced frame core was introduced to reinforce the void that is the courtyard. The eccentric braced frame at the courtyard garden was expressed as a five-story exterior lattice that was encased in pink fiberglass. The organic form counters the rigidity of the stacked volumes that make up the building. Along the boulevard, we pulled several of the units toward the street, to activate the facade, to capture movement and life.

As part of that, we also asked Patrick to explore the idea of a front porch. Two things that are often lacking in facilities built for seniors are a porch and, more generally, social space. We envisioned having porches where the residents could sit in front of their units and talk with people passing by. Everything is thought through in terms of how we can enhance the lives of our tenants who have special needs.

Part of what I have come to learn from this process is that you need to be able to tell a great story about a building when you're pitching it to a community: who it's for, how it's going to help that group, how it's going to contribute to the neighborhood, and, generally, why it makes sense. We thought through the needs of this particular group, and we were able to tell the story of why this building is so important to the community.

For me, it is most exciting to hear the stories of the tenants who end up living in these buildings. They are remarkable. In one of our other buildings, we have a polio victim who previously had been living on the second story of a townhouse. She was on disability and out of that money she had to pay the neighborhood kids to carry her wheelchair up and down the stairs every time she wanted to leave. Otherwise she would literally crawl up and down the stairs to her unit. Well, she won the lottery process to get a new apartment. Now she is in a motorized wheelchair, right next to public transportation, and was able to get a job as an executive assistant. It completely transformed her life. These buildings are so important in terms of the needs they fill.

The courtyard is a special place for the residents, and it gives them a reprieve from the heavy traffic along the boulevard. A series of paths with built-in seating cuts through the central space, and natural light filters through the bamboo. From the courtyard, each of the residents can enter his or her unit. Where buildings usually have balconies that face the ▸

street, Sierra Bonita's private outdoor spaces face the courtyard. By having each unit's front porch overlook the garden, we're encouraging social interaction among the residents and creating a community. The courtyard really is the heart of the project.

The building is being populated through a lottery; there were over 2,000 applicants for the forty-two units. We had many community meetings during the process of designing the project, and as a result there was little opposition. The community members feel proud to be involved; the building also belongs to them. ▸

We worked extremely
hard to make sure that
the design ended up get-
ting built and that the
quality of the project was
sustained through the
process. In that respect,
Sierra Bonita truly was
a labor of love. As an
architect, sometimes you
show up at the job site
and realize that everyone
there is probably getting
paid more than you are.
But in the end, the building is very important and
the user group needs an
advocate. It is my hope
that through the design
of this building, aware-
ness is raised and perhaps
the standard of affordable
housing will be, too.

Stanley Street

Stanley Street Homes
Location Amherst, Massachusetts **Date** Houses 1 and 2 completed 2009 **Client** Pioneer Valley Habitat for Humanity **Client liaison** MJ Adams **Design firm** Kuhn Riddle Architects **Design team** Pooja Khanna, Charles Roberts **Area** Four homes, each 1,150 sq. ft. **Cost** Not available **Estimated value of pro bono design services** $30,000 **Websites** www.pioneervalleyhabitat.org, www.kuhnriddle.com

Charles Roberts
Associate, Kuhn Riddle
Architects,
Amherst, Massachusetts

ARCHITECT

Our firm has worked with Amherst College for a number of years on several projects, mostly renovating old dormitories and offices. We have also done construction drawings for houses designed by other architects for Habitat for Humanity. I did that work because I believe in the organization's cause. I also hoped it could lead to designing a house from the ground up for Habitat.

In its donation of the land for this project, Amherst College stipulated that the houses must be both energy efficient and architecturally significant, challenging the notion of a typical volunteer-built house. Other architects from Kuhn Riddle Architects (KRA) and I attended several vision meetings between Habitat and the college before the final design was approved. For years, Habitat houses have been stick-built, standard construction, with fiberglass ▸

MJ Adams
Executive Director, Pioneer Valley Habitat for Humanity,
Florence, Massachusetts

CLIENT

Our organization, Pioneer Valley Habitat for Humanity, always had a hard time finding land in the college town of Amherst. Homes are very expensive and available land remains at a premium. But because of our location in western Massachusetts, our chapter regularly works with students from Amherst College and other schools in the valley. One student from Amherst, James Tachett, was working with us at a site in Northampton, and after he inquired about it, we took a renewed look at all of the unused property owned by Amherst College.

Once we identified the property that we wanted, James met with the school's president. During the meeting, the president got excited about Habitat's work, at which point James pulled out a list of properties, saying, "We think these three sites have the greatest potential." Apparently the president was taken aback, but he was still excited about the prospects.

Amherst's board of trustees ultimately selected the parcel of land on which we could build four single-family homes. The college was willing to give us this land, but it wanted to make sure the finished project would look nice and blend with and complement the surrounding environment. The site is on the edge of an open meadow and is highly visible in the neighborhood. Habitat's goal, as it is with all of our projects, was to make the homes simple, modest, affordable, and decent. Affordable does not mean it has to be ugly; the design can still be interesting.

Given the way our organization works, whatever was designed had to be able to be built by highly unskilled volunteers. We call that evaluation the "buildability test." The college's leadership encouraged many people who worked for the school, both architects and consultants, to donate their services to us. It was incredibly valuable, and that is really how we made the homes affordable. ▸

batt insulation, gabled roofs, and very simple forms. The designs are easy for volunteers to put together. Getting folks that do not necessarily have construction skills to build these houses is one of the organization's biggest challenges.

It was important to Amherst College, however, that this be a superinsulated building with solar orientation and photovoltaic panels. Because the houses are superinsulated and small, we used a point source heater in each home. It's essentially a wall gas heater that sits downstairs and heats the whole house. There is no ducting and no air-circulation system. It is a very simple, inexpensive system that works for the whole house.

From an architectural point of view, we wanted to incorporate geometric shapes and forms—an agricultural vernacular that I jokingly refer to as "chicken coops." There's a big, abandoned egg farm across the way, and it has a relaxed and familiar combination of sheds and porch roofs. The structure has just three components: the outbuildings, the front porch, and the main house. In our houses, these shapes interlock in an understandable way, but at the same time it is new and different for a residence.

We gave Habitat our drawings, and they built the first house. The volunteer labor missed a couple of details, such as the way some of the siding comes together, the window treatments, and the paint colors. I mentioned ▸

these issues to the team at Habitat, and they asked me to get involved in the paint selections for the next two units.

The houses were originally conceived as being one color with no trim paint. The window trim, the corner boards, and the eaves would all be monolithic, which would make the shapes very sculptural. But that concept was a tough sell. The first house was built the way I had imagined it, a variation on the white farmhouse and red barn, but the stair and storage shed had painted trim. Habitat wanted to paint them in ways that were more intuitively obvious from a vernacular standpoint.

These houses are very prominent in the landscape. A lot of people go by them every day, and many in the community saw them being built. They are happy houses, not the standard, plain, box houses that you see going up everywhere. When you drive by and see them, there is a real awareness of Habitat's work. That alone gives you a good feeling.

The Habitat homes didn't immediately bring KRA any paying clients, but they have brought a lot of good karma. It is evident that the firm is contributing to the community, and the project raises people's awareness of KRA as a design firm that cares about the town. That helps us, whether bringing in work directly or getting us out there in a broader sense.

Kuhn Riddle Architects had worked for Amherst College on a number of projects, and the firm volunteered to design the homes. Chuck Roberts worked with our building committee and structures coordinator to come up with a design. The group looked at many possibilities and landed on one, which is simple, straightforward, and elegant. As a part of the Habitat model, we then engaged the community in the actual construction.

The new homeowners adore the houses. The homes are particularly wonderful because they have light, open floor plans, and optimized solar orientation. There are a lot of windows with southern exposures, which makes it feel like you are outdoors. Our first homeowner, Kathy Perry, is a master gardener and has landscaped her yard, a process that she says has renewed her spirit. The second homeowner, Ashlee Cancio-Bello, moved in after living in a basement for three years. For her, it is extraordinary to be in a home with light and ventilation.

Some people criticize the houses for being too upscale for Habitat for Humanity. We temper that by saying, "They meet the budget requirements; they serve the families that we intended to serve; and we built them with volunteers." The KRA houses truly are beautiful.

The most successful aspect of the project has been community engagement. There are two new families living in attractive and affordable homes in Amherst, and, when the last houses are completed, there will be two more. The new residents feel connected to the town because community members helped build their homes. Thanks to Amherst College, Chuck, and KRA, we ended up with an extraordinary project that has been successful for the families, the college, and for us as a Habitat affiliate.

Tassafaronga

Tassafaronga Village
Location Oakland, California **Date** 2010 **Client** Habitat for Humanity East Bay **Client liaison** Janice Jensen
Design firm David Baker + Partners **Design team** David Baker, Mark Hogan, Peter MacKenzie, Sara Mae
Martens, Amit Price Patel, Daniel Simons, Angela Thomasen **Area** 27,350 sq. ft. **Cost** $5.45 million
Estimated value of pro bono design services $22,000 **Websites** www.habitateb.org,
www.dbarchitect.com

David Baker
Principal, David Baker +
Partners,
San Francisco, California

ARCHITECT

Looking back at the history of public housing in the U.S., much of it was built as cheaply and haphazardly as possible, and it ended up destroying communities in the process. If an area was identified as "blighted," it was torn down and rebuilt. The planning theories employed were based on having large, common, open spaces with segregated uses and lots of parking. Over time, we've learned that doesn't really work.

Tassafaronga is on the site of an isolated, poorly maintained public housing project that had deteriorated. It had been neglected for a long time and most of the units weren't even occupied, so the OHA took the opportunity to start over and create more appropriate building types. Tassafaronga is part of a larger redevelopment effort. There's a new school nearby, as well as a community center. ▸

Janice Jensen
President and CEO, Habitat for Humanity East Bay,
Oakland, California

CLIENT

The Tassafaronga Village site was originally a public housing project, which was home to the poorest of the poor in Oakland. The Oakland Housing Authority (OHA) decided to tear it down and make it a more diverse project for different income levels, and they brought in our Habitat for Humanity affiliate to provide a home-ownership component. Part of our organization's mission is to revitalize neighborhoods, and this was a perfect project to do that.

We try to design our homes to match the neighborhoods in which they will be located. Often that means we come up with a traditional look. This was a unique opportunity, since the neighborhood that OHA was developing is designed to look very modern and chic. In terms of materials, colors, and details, I think our project and the OHA units are very similar, but the massing of ours looks much more like a traditional house. Our decision to organize things that way was part of our attempt to create something sustainable for the community members. We want these houses to look different, but we also want them to fit in—it was a fine line to walk. In the end, we want our homes to have a look of permanence, like someone owns them.

David Baker + Partners brought extensive expertise in affordable housing to the table. The breadth of experience that the firm has and its ability to give examples of what other developers have done in the past was really helpful. The architects that we normally work with typically come from a single-family residential background, as we usually build single-family homes and duplexes. This was our first time building triplexes.

The firm's pro bono contribution made the partnership possible for us. We wouldn't have been able to do this without them. It's been a genuinely happy marriage. In the past, we have had to bring architects up to speed on what our goals are and what we are trying to accomplish. In this case, they already knew and understood our mission and methods. ▸

When we got the program from Habitat for Humanity, it simply asked us to provide a certain number of units, with a certain amount of parking, and a certain unit mix. The larger, three-unit buildings we developed were beyond what Habitat was used to; the whole site was tight, and there wasn't as much parking as many of the organization's other sites have.

This is dense, urban housing, and we got a lot more bang for our buck in this project by having common spaces, rather than trying to maximize private open space. The common spaces are not completely open to the public; residents have some ownership over them. That was one of the problems with the previous site, where there was a lot of indefensible space. We also took a lot of care to make sure that the sidewalks are good, that there's plenty of planting, and that front doors face the street. We didn't want to design something that, when people saw it, they thought, "There's that housing project with all the weird buildings."

Habitat for Humanity does energy and materially efficient building, and this project would probably qualify for LEED gold or platinum certification. The organization has a lot of sustainability targets built into the guidelines that it gives all of its architects and engineers when they start a new project. We took those goals even further with Tassafaronga. The leaders at Habitat made a deal with Pacific Gas & Electric on photovoltaic ▸

Tassafaronga is slightly more modern than other projects we've done. It was the first time that we did an open plan on the first floor, for example. We have very specific guidelines from Habitat for Humanity International that call for a simple, decent home, which translates as "not too large," so it was really nice to have an open first floor with an efficient kitchen. It overlaps with the living areas and creates spaces where people can meet and gather.

We mandate that our homes must be simple to build. Working with architects can be a challenge because we primarily use volunteer labor for construction. That is our main motivation for adhering to the design criteria. It's something we articulate to the design consultants, and it is something we tell our applicants, so they know what they are getting when they buy a Habitat home. Our project architect at David Baker's office paid special attention to these constraints, while still coming up with some creative detailing.

Our design team was especially helpful in the LEED Neighborhood Development process; we had never done it before. We have a pretty high standard for green construction already, but we didn't have experience with the planning process. There are three different building types in Tassafaronga, and our plan right now is to certify one of each type for LEED for Homes. All of them are going to get Green Point and Energy Star certifications, making this one of our greenest developments to date.

solar panels, so we're using solar thermal arrays for hot water.

In addition to its green building principles, Habitat for Humanity has a very systematic way of putting its buildings together. There are a limited number of window sizes, and there are constraints on framing. This is partly to make the building as efficient as possible but also because the organization needs to make construction simple. Lay people, including the families who will live in the houses, provide most of the labor, almost all on a volunteer basis. We had a lot of discussion about developing our techniques to work better within that system.

One advantage to this kind of work is that it broadens your horizons. You tend to get very specialized in architecture; not that it is boring, but it can get stale. The 1% program of Public Architecture and pro bono design work generally are good ways of working around that.

John Cary

The following pages outline the ways in which nonprofit organizations—art galleries, camps, community and health centers, housing providers, libraries, schools, and others—can become informed clients. They also frame how architecture firms can most strategically invest their creativity and time, how funders can make lasting investments in order to help the causes they care about most reach their greatest potential, and how manufacturers can put their best products to work for the public good.

Architects, like other professionals, have created a language all their own. However, while the terminology belonging to the legal, medical, and other professions has made its way into common parlance, architecture terminology has done so to a much lesser extent. Architects have coined terms that express one thing in the context of architectural practice but mean something entirely different in other realms, including the nonprofit sector. For instance, in the architecture world, a basic word like "program" means the scope of work and needs, while in the nonprofit world, it means a type of activity an organization undertakes to advance its mission. Thus, clear communication between architects and their clients is essential.

Architecture and design professionals also sometimes use specialized terms, foreign to those outside the design bubble, to describe the phases most architectural projects go through: pre-design, conceptual or schematic design, design development, construction documents, and construction administration. In the simplest of terms, pre-design is the moment to assess the needs of a client, understand the group's ability to raise money, and build the support it needs. Conceptual or schematic design is where those needs start to take shape, often with sketches, diagrams, renderings, or even models, which can become useful tools in a capital campaign, for example. Design development is when issues like the size of rooms and types of materials are determined, while construction documents look at those decisions down to the smallest detail. Construction administration is the role an architect assumes when a contractor brings the design to life.

Min | Day
Bemis Art Center,
Omaha, Nebraska.
Rendering

Each of the built projects in this book successfully navigated these issues and phases. Many of the ways in which they and others have done so are synthesized here into a series of recommendations, which clients, firms, funders, and manufacturers are encouraged to consider as they embark on pro bono projects and partnerships.

Pro Bono Clients

The scene of a nonprofit crammed into an uninspiring space that matches neither its services nor its ambitions is replayed countless times across the country in community centers, health clinics, libraries, arts organizations, and other settings. For some, their shabby space is a point of pride and seen as a demonstration of the group's need. But it can also be seen as representative of the organization's expectations. If that space discourages people from volunteering and leads to high staff turnover, even the most affordable or fully donated space becomes a liability, not an asset. This section—in fact, this entire book—is written with the firm belief that an organization's space can and should be one of its greatest assets. It should be representative of the change the nonprofit is working to make in the world. It is possible. And, when done well, that improved physical space will be admired and respected by the organization's clients, staff, volunteers, funders, and patrons alike.

The vast majority of nonprofits, with the exception of organizations like schools and libraries, have never engaged the services of an architect. Unlike accountants and attorneys, very few architects serve on the boards of directors of nonprofits, for example. Even nonprofits that undertake major capital campaigns or facility renovations that require architectural services will do so just once or twice in their history. Thus, there needs to be crystal clear communication about expectations and roles, as well as how architectural projects work, how long they can take, and what kinds of actual costs might be involved in the short and long term.

The most successful partnerships in this book relied on a high level of feedback and co-education between the client and designer. Matt Hathorne of Hathorne Architects in Detroit attended a summer camp for children with autism before working on a renovation for the Judson Center Autism Connections. He noted that overstimulated children would hide under tables draped with blankets to re-center themselves. This experience directly informed his design when he added small nooks to the classroom walls for the kids to get much-needed alone time, while still remaining within view of the teachers.

Beyond the pride that comes with a new or renovated space, there are also significant organizational benefits that align closely with activities common to almost every type of nonprofit, regardless of its mission, focus, or even size. Some of the areas that design can aid include capacity building, fund-raising and development, awareness raising, branding, and recruitment and retention of clients, staff, supporters, and volunteers.

Good design "builds capacity," as the practice is widely called in the nonprofit and philanthropic sectors, by enabling an organization to deliver more services to more people without requiring a comparable increase in resources. From developing better storage to scrutinizing workflow, thoughtful design simply allows people to do more. Rethinking existing facilities is often the simplest way in which design can have a profound impact, and sometimes the outcome is the realization that an organization's existing space is perfectly sufficient.

Nonprofits do not have to know everything that they want out of their facilities before they begin, but they do need to commit to asking and answering some fundamental questions: Where are they going as an organization? What are their immediate and future needs? What are the obstacles, physical and otherwise, that will limit progress? What are the steps necessary to overcome these limita-tions? What is a realistic timeline? Designers can interpret and help nonprofits

understand how their current facilities affect their answers to these questions. Likewise, designers involved early in the process can help identify resources and suggest ways that design can be a powerful tool to achieve the client's goals.

A critical first step for a client is simply to look at how the organization functions in its space. How do its patients, staff, volunteers, and other visitors relate to the space? Which areas need to be private and which ones public? What are the most highly trafficked areas? Is there any unutilized space? Architects have an innate ability to help clients answer these questions, and they can provide objective assessments, free of the assumptions and biases commonly established over time. In designing the headquarters for Hands On Atlanta, Jova/Daniels/Busby used a mapping system to track how spaces were populated throughout the day. This allowed the architects to assess which areas needed to be public, private, or mixed-use.

It is important for the staff, board, and other users of the facility to articulate the trajectory and ambitions of the organization. Design that anticipates this evolution will lead to a space solution that stands the test of time, particularly if it is adaptable. Again, Hands On Atlanta provides a potent example. Its national organization, Hands On Network, merged with another national nonprofit, the Points of Light Foundation, which was then located in Washington, D.C. The assumption by many in the service field was that the national headquarters of the newly constituted Points of Light Institute would be located in D.C., but Hands On Atlanta's new facility was so impressive and adaptable that it made more sense to house the newly enlarged entity, now one of the largest volunteer organizations in the country, there.

New buildings, renovations, and other capital projects also offer opportunities to energize current donors and engage prospective partners. Project milestones can be used to develop corresponding fund-raising strategies that actively involve

left and opposite
Richard H. Lewis Architect
P.S. 47,
Bronx, New York, 2009

donors in each construction phase. People naturally gravitate to dynamic organizations where positive change and growth are afoot. Tangible, physical advances get donors invested in the development of an organization in a way that annual appeals or call drives rarely do. Highlighting the relationship between an organization's mission and the design project will create buzz and catalyze the involvement of other supporters. When nonprofits work to solicit input from donors and the larger community, those individuals will feel they had a role in shaping the organization and will be more likely to support it in the future.

Studio Gang designed the Lavezzorio Community Center in Chicago for SOS Children's Villages Illinois, an organization that reunites foster children with their biological family members, and provides care for children and families who have endured difficult circumstances. The organization had long wanted to enhance and support its local community by offering services such as day care, but it did not have space to make that happen. The collaboration between the architect and client allowed SOS Illinois to meet that goal, and the building has become the anchor of the community because of the many committed people who were involved in its development.

Renovations, new construction, and even initial capital campaigns to achieve these ends can generate broad interest in the community. One approach to building this involvement is to actively draw key community members' attention to new plans and programs by inviting them to visit the site during various stages of the project. Nonprofits can develop a brief and informal script that supporters and board and staff members can use to highlight compelling design features and explain how their project will improve the way the organization operates. The team should consider what visuals and talking points will most clearly express the most interesting parts of the project and prominently display this information on presentation boards. Organizations should also include regular updates about the work in their newsletters and donor mailings and on their websites.

Staff, users, or other occupants of the planned space should spend time thinking about the organization, how it is perceived, and how it would like to be perceived. Architects can then be enlisted to discuss how to make the experience of the space itself convey these values. They can consider, for instance, how natural light can be used to lift moods, how windows facing the street can increase transparency, and how color and material choices can convey energy, authenticity, and openness. They can even go a step further, unifying these ideas into a coherent brand that is expressed across the organization's communications materials, website, and building signage.

For instance, the L!brary Initiative brought on graphic designer Michael Beirut to develop the program's signage, including the "!" in L!brary. This single element unified the fifty-six projects, which were completed by nearly two dozen design firms, each with its own design aesthetic. In addition, the walls of many of the Robin Hood libraries were adorned with portraits—cartoons, drawings, and photographs—of the students at the school. The Goodwill Fillmore Street Store in San Francisco, designed by McCall Design Group, did the same, with larger-than-life murals of local community members, establishing a visual and human connection with each individual who enters the store, which is a significant part of Goodwill's mission and work.

Internally, pro bono clients should make sure they have the support of their boards and staff early on in the process. It is critical to solicit input from staff, volunteers, and other users as a vision for a new space is developed. The people who work in and utilize the space each day will understand the requirements and functional limitations better than anyone, and they will appreciate being consulted as experts.

Employees at nonprofits tend to wear multiple hats. As p:ear director Beth Burns says, "We have such a small staff, that we are both the janitorial service and the people who wear suits and ask for money." That level of flexibility can be reflected in the space by creating multipurpose areas that can adapt to the group's particular needs at any given time. It is also crucial for pro bono clients to identify the key decision-makers within their organizations. Unclear or poorly managed decision-making is the most common, and often the most costly, error in capital projects.

Getting ready for a project means taking an honest look at an organization's resources. A pro bono client's board and staff need to assess whether or not they have—or can secure—the financial and other resources required to build and maintain the project. Pro bono clients can work with their architects to formulate schedules that will allow time to raise the funds. For the Roosevelt Park Master Plan, uRbanDetail and its collaborators have staged the project to include fund-raising after each section is completed. This way the community can experience the park firsthand and also see its potential for growth.

Before the project is under way, a pro bono client should work with its firm to determine the value of its donation. The investment of time and the estimated value of donated services should be agreed upon by both parties and should reflect the scope of work and the goals of the project. The single-most important thing that nonprofits can do to help ensure a successful project is to develop a clear understanding of the roles and responsibilities of each party. It is strongly recommended that this agreement be in writing, and some states even require written agreements on pro bono projects. It is also important to reach an understanding of who will cover what are traditionally reimbursable expenses for design firms (printing, models, travel, etc.), which involve out-of-pocket expenses. Pro bono clients and firms should also develop contingency plans, outlining who will cover costs in the event the work exceeds the budget.

Given that they are donating their time and professional services, in their contracts, firms may ask for reasonable conditions that can assist them in reducing their liability. Basic issues such as scope of services, waiver of claims, indemnification, reimbursement, cost overruns, copyright, and terms of termination may be addressed in a contract provided by the firm offering its services. All contracts should be reviewed with the client's board and legal counsel, and many law firms can provide such services.

Design firms are there to apply their knowledge to help nonprofits meet their goals. At every stage of the project, the firm and the pro bono client should understand the potential pros and cons associated with their joint design choices. The firm's donation should not be considered limitless, however. Even if the work is being done gratis, pro bono clients should expect to receive invoices on a regular basis noting time spent and the value of the donation. They can use the invoices to track where they are in the budget and the services that are being provided.

In pro bono relationships, it is extremely important for all parties, but particularly the staff and members of the nonprofit, to offer thanks and recognition to those providing assistance. The architects donating their time deserve to be treated like any donor at a comparable level. Press and public acknowledgments, as well as invitations to programs and events, are but a few ways to highlight a firm's contributions. In many of the projects featured in this book, the architects have gone on to act as board members for the organizations they assisted.

Good design creates places that engage people, enable staff and volunteers to work better, and help occupants thrive. It makes nonprofits stronger and can uniquely advance their causes. Organizations need to know that design resources are within their reach to help fulfill their missions.

Pro Bono Architects

Pro bono service can easily be seen as a one-way street, but that perspective ignores the many benefits firms can reap from these partnerships. They include opportunities for heightened creativity, recruitment and retention of employees and clients, local involvement and deepened community relations, and personal satisfaction.

Pro bono projects allow firms to exercise their best creative abilities. Some architects' most creative work emerges from the positive friction introduced by new project types and unfamiliar programs. Likewise, pro bono projects can become portfolio pieces that help firms gain entry to new design markets. After its pro bono work for the Calvin Hill School, Lisa Gray of Gray Organschi Architecture saw her firm's focus broaden from predominantly high-end residential projects to include early childhood educational facilities.

Some of the firms represented in this book were built on pro bono work. Scott | Edwards Architecture of Portland, Oregon, has worked on over thirty pro bono projects since opening in 1997. For its first job, the firm built a dental clinic for the nonprofit Virginia Garcia Memorial Health Center to serve migrant farmers and the uninsured throughout rural Oregon. Since then, Scott | Edwards has completed ten projects for the organization. "I've got a lot of clients who just pass my name on, and that's resulted in a lot of work with nonprofit groups," says principal Sid Scott. "I see it as a tremendous market. It makes a lot of sense from a business standpoint."[1] The partnership has been successful for the nonprofit as well: Virginia Garcia has since grown to be the premier healthcare provider for low-income residents of central Oregon.

Others have seen pro bono work as a way to weather the recent recession. Studio G Architects, based outside of Boston, saw its revenue drop in 2008 with

opposite
Studio Gang Architects
Lavezzorio Community Center,
Chicago, Illinois. 2008

right and far right
Studio G Architects
Massachusetts Affordable Housing Alliance,
Dorchester, Massachusetts. 2006

ten planned projects placed on hold or abandoned altogether. Rather than immediately cut staff, principal Gail Sullivan instructed her employees to dedicate fifteen to twenty hours per week to pro bono work in the hopes of attracting new clients. In short order, her firm secured funding for a number of projects. As Sullivan told the *Wall Street Journal*, "Offering the pro bono services has given us a chance to maintain our design vigor and resulted in people hiring us."[2]

Matt Hathorne started his practice just as the recession struck, drying up the pool of potential clients. Instead of abandoning the new firm, Hathorne decided to offer schematic design services pro bono to nonprofits through a local newsletter. The Judson Center Autism Connections facility was his studio's first completed project. It afforded the firm critical experience, built work for its portfolio, media exposure, and a great client reference. Similarly, Stephen Dalton of Stephen Dalton Architects took on the Hanna Fenichel Center for Child Development as his first client, winning multiple design awards and building the firm's portfolio to capture future work.

Despite these and many other instances of pro bono projects generating new business, most firms turn to design competitions with the belief that they are creative outlets that can lead to new work. However, with only one winner and potentially dozens, hundreds, or thousands of entries, the efforts of the vast majority are wasted. Public Architecture's founder, architect John Peterson, is among the more vocal critics of design competitions. Instead of entering a competition during a slow period in the office, he and the staff of his firm decided to identify a design opportunity closer to home, right outside the office walls. The project, a proposal to creatively integrate more public spaces into a former light-industrial zone in San Francisco (an image of it leads off the Community section of this book), generated more press and interest than any paying project taken on by the firm before or since.

One of the most progressive firms when it comes to institutionalizing a culture of pro bono work is Perkins+Will. With over twenty offices around the world and completed projects in forty-three countries, Perkins+Will became the first large firm in the U.S. to craft a company-wide policy on pro bono service. That policy called for the allocation of 1 percent of each employee's working hours to pro bono service. This mandate led to the establishment of the firm's Social Responsibility Initiative (SRI), which coordinates all of its pro bono work.

Each office of Perkins+Will now has a dedicated SRI officer, supervised by the managing partner of that office, and overseen by a national committee and national partners. In May 2009, Perkins+Will marked another first: becoming the first design firm to publish a report on its pro bono pursuits. The report was circulated to employees, published on the firm's website, and made available to clients. Such publications are common practice among law firms but were until then nonexistent in the architecture profession. In this case, it documented works-in-progress in Perkins+Will's numerous offices, including a resource center for homeless people, a skateboarding park in the Chicago area, a design concept for a music school in New Orleans, the renovation of the Tenement Museum in Manhattan, as well as an exhibition at the New York City Police Museum. It gave the firm something tangible that every employee could feel a part of and could point to. And it gave every other architecture firm a model to build on as they share and promote their pro bono work.

A key to getting the most out of a pro bono project and making it a valuable exercise for the firm is to set high design expectations for the client, the project, and the design team. Firms should start with the goal that each pro bono project be an important addition to their portfolios. As its largely retail client base dried up during the 2008 recession, the McCall Design Group took on an inner-city museum and school, and in the process, added two new project types to its portfolio. Firms must also be deliberate in selecting clients who appreciate

and share their creative goals, and they can do so by clearly articulating those goals for their potential partners. Studio Gang's award-winning design work for the Chinese American Service League and SOS Children's Villages Illinois are prime examples of this.

Firms do need to be selective and strategic in choosing pro bono projects, articulating to their employees how decisions about taking on that work are made. To vet project opportunities, firms should consider forming a committee that is representative of their structure and values. Perkins+Will's dedicated SRI officers field project requests and identify opportunities, which are then presented for consideration.

Many firms, such as David Baker + Partners in San Francisco, SERA Architects of Portland, Oregon, and Jova/Daniels/Busby of Atlanta, use pro bono work as a way of mentoring younger designers on their staffs and allowing them to spearhead their own projects. Others have found more innovative ways of structuring the work internally. San Francisco's EHDD organized an in-office competition for the design of an outdoor seating area on the grounds of the Randall Museum, a natural history museum with a spectacular view of the city skyline. The firm had a jury of past clients, local politicians, and museum employees rate the designs and select the one that would be detailed and built.

Projects that advance employees' interests and passions can be excellent motivators and deliver real satisfaction. Pro bono projects give firms a chance to engage and inspire every employee—design and non-design staff members alike. HOK's design for an animal shelter in St. Louis was instigated by the firm's IT director, Penny Malina, who, as architects have moved in and out, has provided continuity for the project. There are also opportunities to bring employees together at key points in a project to celebrate successes and milestones, using these gatherings as moments to remind everyone of the firm's commitment to social values and desire to make significant contributions to the public good.

Local pro bono projects can strengthen ties and build relationships in the community. Additionally, many pro bono projects provide opportunities for collaborations with artists, government agencies, suppliers, and even other firms. Employees may also appreciate seeing tangible results of their work, which can be difficult for midsize and large firms that are commissioned to do work far from where they practice. Often the best and most relevant projects are found in one's backyard. They provide opportunities to enlist business leaders, community activists, government officials, and others who have a vested interest in the work and the surrounding neighborhood.

Advocating for a cause is an effective way to demonstrate a firm's values and to send a signal of a healthy and mature business. When people see a firm mobilizing its talents for the public good, they will seek out its services and share its story with others. Cause-based projects also generate outside interest from the media. Many of the projects in this book won local, regional, and national design awards. Among them are the Hanna Fenichel Center for Child Development by Stephen Dalton Architects, which received the national AIA Small Project Award, and the Robin Hood L!brary Initiative, which has received awards from the AIA, the American Library Association, and others.

Some of the most compelling project examples and profiles in this book involve architects becoming advocates for their client's missions and causes. San Francisco architect Anne Fougeron of Fougeron Architecture has partnered with Planned Parenthood for more than fifteen years, completing over a dozen projects of varying scales. The work they have done together is an integral part of the firm's portfolio as well as her own level of satisfaction on the job. Firms should encourage their employees to delve deeper into the causes for which

they have chosen to work. They should also consider how the firm can add value to those causes, and understand that realizations stemming from pro bono projects can inform and shape their future fee-generating work as well.

Firms can also meet with their client's development staff and offer to get their message out to the professional design community or consider hosting informational or fund-raising events in their offices and invite colleagues and community leaders. At a minimum, they can send press releases to relevant media and add updates aimed at generating excitement about the project's progress to their websites.

Pro bono projects create opportunities for designers to make a difference in people's lives as well as experience the impact that difference makes. The work can end up being some of the most rewarding of an architect's career. Just as pro bono work is an investment in the community, being a part of positive change offers contributors a deep sense of personal satisfaction.

While being interviewed for this book, Seattle architect Rick Sundberg of Olson Kundig Architects, described his pro bono work to be both creatively and intellectually expansive.[3] The budget and material constraints have opened him up to design challenges that are absent from the high-end projects his firm typically works on. He plans to dedicate 50 percent of his time to pro bono work in the coming years.

Many firms' catch-as-catch-can attitude toward pro bono work—if it is addressed at all—can make project management difficult. One way to alleviate or avoid this problem is to include all principals and decision-makers in considering what causes, organizations, and projects to commit to. This is important so that the firm has unity and consensus and brings its full expertise and usual delivery protocols to the project. Firms must also assess their resources and review

current and upcoming projects to determine whether or not they have available talent and bandwidth. They should take an honest, but generous, look at their short-term workloads and finances to determine the number of hours they can realistically commit to each project. After firms determine the resources they can offer, they can select projects that fit within those parameters. Whether doing initial needs assessments or providing full architectural services, selecting projects that match available resources will minimize staffing issues down the road.

But all decisions are not settled at the outset of a project. Firms must continue to assess more fundamental issues, such as the client's ability to realize the project. Do the organization's resources match its goals and timeline? Will the primary decision-makers be around for the duration of the project? If the client's goals are, or even feel, unrealistic, firms have every right and some amount of responsibility to assist the nonprofit in setting new goals or forgoing the project entirely.

A clear budget and schedule to track resources spent on the project are essential. Firms are encouraged to produce invoices as they would for any project and submit them to their clients, tracking the hours spent against the time budgeted, but reflecting a zero balance—as well as showing both the market value and reduced rate on the invoice. In consultation with the clients, firms should also develop contingency plans for issues such as who will cover costs in the event that the project exceeds the agreed upon budget, as well as more incidental costs, like those that are out-of-pocket for the firm or typically reimbursibles.

In the early years of Public Architecture's The 1% program, junior employees and senior principals alike skeptically broached with us the issue of liability. There is a perception that in donating their time, firms should be absolved of liability exposure. While the short answer is that firms remain equally liable whether they are paid or not, every major provider of insurance to architecture firms has provisions for pro bono projects. Firms should consult their insurance carriers about this, but the best way to manage their exposure to liability is to choose their clients and projects carefully. The second thing they can do is sign a written contract before work begins. Although a pro bono project may not involve any exchange of money, all parties need to make clear, in writing, their mutual expectations and understandings. A contract is ultimately advantageous for all parties. It is important to understand that while there are no special exemptions from liability for pro bono projects, there are reasonable requests that firms can make to limit their exposure.

All of these practical matters aside, being an architect is about much more than a job. It's about contributing to the social, environmental, and economic health of our society. Pro bono is an outlet to do just that. It's the act of putting one's professional skills to work for the greater good. The need has never been greater. There are millions of deserving people and organizations that could benefit from pro bono design. These needs will always be there, and this is why pro bono design is so important and so powerful.

Pro Bono Project Funders

The dilemma that plagues pro bono projects is how to get them funded. Foundations are notorious for turning away requests for capital projects and are even less interested in facility maintenance costs. And yet foundations and some of our country's greatest philanthropists have long been associated with well-designed buildings and spaces, be they on college campuses or in inner cities.

Between the late 1800s and the early 1900s, Andrew Carnegie commissioned and built over 1,600 libraries throughout the United States and almost that many elsewhere around the world. More recently, major foundations have invested in similar capital projects. The Rockefeller Foundation's office in New York was one of the first commercial interior projects designed by architect Maya Lin, who is perhaps best known for her design of the Vietnam Memorial in Washington, D.C.

The McKnight Foundation office in Minneapolis, designed by Meyer, Scherer & Rockcastle (the architects behind the Alvar Street Branch Library, which is featured in the Community section of this book), is a wood-filled space in a renovated flour mill overlooking the Mississippi River and a model example of adaptive reuse.

In the foundation world, one of the foremost leaders when it comes to understanding the impact of facilities is the Kresge Foundation. Based outside of Detroit, Kresge is backed by nearly $3 billion in assets originating from a major gift around the turn of the twentieth century from the business that evolved into Kmart. The foundation understands the value of design, evidenced by its own headquarters, a high-performance green building designed by the Chicago-based Valerio Dewalt Train Associates. Kresge presents its "facilities capital grants" as supporting the "acquisition and construction of facilities, including land, new construction and existing property renovation, and major equipment purchases." It typically awards these grants on a matching basis, challenging other donors to support the cause. Kresge's expressed priority areas are, in fact, very similar to those of most other foundations: "health, the environment, community development, arts and culture, education and human services."[4] But it addresses those interests in large part through capital grants, thus building capacity in organizations that concentrate on those areas.

Whether champions of the environment, education, health, or other issues, foundations and funders are focused on maximizing the impact of their investments and helping to grow the organizations they deem worthy of their support. Meanwhile the potential of virtually every nonprofit is influenced in significant ways by the space that it inhabits—the space where its clients come for services, where its volunteers donate their time, and where other donors come to see their work in action.

The reality, though, is that "bricks and mortar" or "bricks and sticks" grants, as capital gifts are often called, are routinely eschewed by the foundation world.

The reasons for this are difficult to pin down, but in conversation with a small number of foundation leaders, we have come to understand some of the thinking behind this position. One leader noted "perceived leverage," viewing capital projects as having inherently less impact than program support. Others described such giving as "conservative grant-making," typically reserved for big institutions, like universities or museums, where a family or foundation name on a building is a status symbol. Yet the single-greatest concern expressed was about cost: Buildings are expensive to construct and expensive to maintain.

This book sheds new light on the strength of architectural design as an investment that yields great returns in a variety of ways. These returns start during the design process, which is inherently collaborative and rests on the ability of the design team to bring the nonprofit, local government, and local citizenry together to work toward a common solution. No facility, no matter how well intentioned, will be successful without the involvement of each of these partners.

Nonprofits dedicated to serving society's dispossessed can sometimes find themselves ostracized, pushed to the edges of a community. A new building or even a well-considered renovation can reposition the organization squarely in the public consciousness, leading to new appreciation of the causes and issues that the group is working to address. This strengthens the cause, its supporters, and those who are affected by it.

At its core, the practice of design is about doing more with less. Understanding how to maximize human, capital, physical, and organizational resources for the greatest real-world use is design's great contribution to the needs of nonprofits. If donors and foundations are constantly striving to understand the ripple effect their grants have, and trying to squeeze the most out of every dollar they are privileged to give away, design represents one of the soundest investments they can make.

Foundations and donors have an opportunity to plant their flags in institutions that, if well vetted and supported, won't be moving on any time soon. This can be seen as a massive vote of confidence in the nonprofit and the community that it supports. In a time when longevity and sustainability are seen as adding value, ensuring that disadvantaged communities have access to the same healthy environments and standards of design and construction that many of us enjoy is paramount.

Architects and their pro bono clients have the expertise to make projects successful once they are under way, but funders can be vitally important in ensuring that the groundwork is laid well. Even if monetary backing is limited, funders can identify other resources that organizations can look to for support. They can assist the organization in defining its goals for the project and plan for future growth and changes. They can also aid nonprofits in understanding the opportunities and challenges associated with a new facility.

Material Donations

Whether they produce chairs, flooring, lighting, or other fixtures, every major manufacturer in the building industry makes the materials and furnishings essential to create functional, comfortable, appealing spaces for everyone, including organizations that rely on pro bono design. Unlike the professional services of architects and designers, in-kind and material donations are 100 percent tax-deductible, providing a major incentive to manufacturers to give.

One manufacturer, Steelcase, has not just furnished but actually undertaken a number of pro bono design projects, in which their in-house design teams tackle every aspect of the jobs. A prime example is the West Michigan Center for Arts and Technology (WMCAT), located in Steelcase's hometown of Grand Rapids.

WMCAT provides classes ranging from arts education to computer training, linking positive social change and economic progress by helping adults develop technical skills. Steelcase contributed its in-house design and facilities groups to the project and donated all of the furnishings for the entire center. The result is a state-of-the-art facility.

Not every manufacturer has the opportunity or the resources for such an endeavor, but all of them routinely have new products that they want to place, photograph, and even test. They also have research and development products, end of lease take-backs, and surplus inventories. Meanwhile nine out of every ten nonprofits in this country are operating out of poorly furnished facilities.

The YWCA project designed by HOK on the south side of Chicago attracted massive amounts of donated materials, while others were made available to the project at-cost. Manufacturers such as AllSteel, Interface Carpets, and U.S. Gypsum all chipped in. The Alvar Street Branch Library also benefited from substantial material donations, including flooring and components of the bookshelves.

Like manufacturers, contractors frequently have a great deal to give and have the same tax deductions associated with their material donations. The architecture firm of ECI/Hyer, in its work on the Camp Kushtaka cabins, and Gensler, in the development of its Eco Cabins at Camp Emerald Bay, effectively utilized materials made available by their contractors, including enormous steel shipping containers in the latter case. In the Halcyon Playhouse for Court Appointed Special Advocates of Northwest Arkansas, architect Walter Jennings planned his design around the materials his contractor had available for free, including metal screens that were left over from a previous project, as well as salvaged plywood.

Buy-in at all levels of the company—from local sales reps far removed from the corporate headquarters to senior executives in the home office—will make a sustainable and enduring commitment, rather than a one-off venture. Like architecture firms donating their services, manufacturers need to be strategic in their donations of materials, clearly defining goals that advance the company's values—high-quality design, low environmental impact, and so on. These goals might best be aligned with their market interests (corporate, residential, institutional, etc.), or they may be in totally new, uncharted areas. Geography is also something to take into consideration: Is the company primarily interested in reinvesting in its local community? Only where it has showrooms? Or just anywhere need exists?

There are numerous ways that a manufacturer can remain involved after making a donation of goods or materials. It can be on-call to supply replacement parts on chairs and workstations, floor, wall, and ceiling panels, and the like. Company leaders can also join the boards of nonprofits whose causes they care about, as Steelcase has done with WMCAT.

A Call to Action

The client-architect relationships represented in this book offer both models and methods for pro bono partnerships to reach their full potential. We hope they encourage nonprofits to imagine the spaces that their important causes deserve and that they motivate architects to offer their services. Someday, in the foreseeable future, a nonprofit leader who used to work in a poorly lit, uninspiring space will lean back in his chair, look around his bright, clean office, and see his staff hard at work. The space will be everything he dreamed of and more—a space that literally and figuratively enacts his vision. Meanwhile a young architect previously disenchanted by her work will see her first pro bono client's vision taking shape. Her nervous excitement about their next meeting will be palpable, as she knows what she's doing truly matters and makes a difference.

Each of the dozens of clients featured in this book also represents the willingness of funders to support the creation of better environments and of manufacturers to furnish them. We hope a foundation program officer will read these pages and convince his colleagues of the value of design as a reliable means to advance the organizations and issues they care about. We hope a local sales representative for a major furniture manufacturer will consider the ways her company's products can benefit nonprofits and people in need, even if they've learned to live without them. In the process, she will put her company's products to work for the public good. Pro bono.

[1] Sid Scott, interview with Cali Pfaff, Nov. 2009.
[2] Raymond Flandez, "Pro Bono Work Helps Firms Fight Economic Slump," *Wall Street Journal*, Sept. 1, 2009.
[3] Rick Sundberg, interview with Brad Leibin, Nov. 2009.
[4] www.kresge.org/index.php/what/index.

John Cary

There are numerous people—collaborators, contributors, colleagues, sponsors, supporters, mentors, friends, and family—to thank for their roles, large and small, in helping me realize *The Power of Pro Bono*.

This book could not have happened without the vision and determination of Diana Murphy at Metropolis Books. The creative dialogue that we have shared has enriched the project significantly. Diana and copy editor Meghan Conaton tirelessly refined and revised the text into its present state. Many people at Distributed Art Publishers and Metropolis Books worked behind the scenes, and I thank all of them for believing in this project.

In July 2009, Diana and I walked into the Fifth Avenue offices of Pentagram for a meeting with graphic designer Paula Scher. Ten minutes into our pitch, Paula told us, "My pro bono projects are my favorite projects," something we would hear time and again throughout our interviews for this book. This beautiful book was skillfully designed by Paula and her dedicated team at Pentagram: Sarah Cohen, Julia Kind, and Lisa Kitschenberg.

Majora Carter's foreword is a powerful manifesto for architecture as a social act, and I am extremely grateful for her contribution to this project. Her words are most worthy to introduce the dozens of client and architect stories featured in the book. None of these organization leaders or designers accomplished their work alone, so I thank them as well as their many collaborators and colleagues, including those who gathered material for publication here.

I thank John Peterson for trusting me to direct Public Architecture throughout the organization's formative years, and for his ongoing investment of ideas, time, and resources since its establishment. Thanks are also due to past and present Public Architecture board members, including Tim Culvahouse, Julie Eizenberg, Rob Forbes, Larry Fried, Ted Landsmark, David Meckel, Chris Parsons, Steve Privett, Fei Tsen, Billie Tsien, Peter Walker, Laura Weiss, Allison Williams, and Tod Williams. Beyond these vital supporters, Public Architecture's most humbling asset is the massive network of firms and nonprofits that are part of The 1% program. We acknowledge and applaud every one of them for their dedication and generosity.

I am indebted to Public Architecture staff members Brad Leibin, Nick McClintock, Cali Pfaff, and Amy Ress as well as volunteers Barbara Franzoia and Ruth Keffer, all of whom contributed extensively to this book, while Liz Ogbu, Mia Scharphie, and others provided consistent feedback. The client/architect perspectives represented in "How to Pro Bono" were informed by the writing that Jeremy Mende of MendeDesign and Public Architecture undertook through our first grant from the Ideas That Matter program of Sappi Limited.

A nimble team of volunteers assisted with conducting, transcribing, and editing the scores of interviews represented in these pages. They include Janine Balistreri, Genevieve Bantle, Heera Bassi, Renee Bissell, Caitlin Cameron, Roselle Curwen, Jacob Day, Taylor Dietrich, Trudy Garber, Gisela Garett, Fred Goykhman, Kelly Gregory, Cat Gutierrez, Meghan Hade, Vaishali Katyarmal, Ruth Keffer, Tasha Leverette, Fabiana Meacham, Michelle Nermon, Celeste Novak, Michael Pearce, Stephanie Sybrandt, Laurel

Stone, Melissa Hill Threatt, Heather Tipton, and Bess Weyandt.

Every effort of Public Architecture is supported by loyal sponsors, be they corporations, foundations, or private individuals. The National Endowment for the Arts, particularly Susan Begley, Maurice Cox, and Jeff Speck, provided the first grant to The 1% program and continued support over the years. Deep gratitude also goes out to supporters such as Sara Davis of the Adobe Foundation, Erica Stoller of Esto Photographics, Claudine Brown and Lance Lindblom of the Nathan Cummings Foundation, Phil Harrison of Perkins+Will, Sunny Fischer of the Driehaus Foundation, Tom Layton of the Gerbode Foundation, and Linda Marston-Reid and Pilar Palacia of the Rockefeller Foundation.

Jennifer Busch and John Rouse of Contract magazine took a leap of faith when they recognized John Peterson and me with the 2009 Designer of the Year Award, thus opening many doors. Among them were substantial gestures of support from the commercial manufacturing community, embodied in lasting relationships with Jon Strassner of Humanscale, Mary Ellen Magee and Maxine Mann of Teknion, John Newland of Herman Miller, and John Stephens of Shaw Contract Group, who secured a substantial, multiyear donation of 1 percent of sales on Shaw's Homage carpet line to support The 1% program. Collectively they have expanded our network and thus the reach of this book.

The pro bono movement, represented here, is a component of the broader public-interest design field, which is led by numerous influential colleagues. They include Bryan Bell of Design Corps, Story Bellows of the Mayors' Institute on City Design, John Bielenberg of Project M, Monica Chadha of Studio Gang, Beth Miller of the Community Design Collaborative, Emily Pilloton of Project H, John Ochsendorf of MIT, Sergio Palleroni of the Building Sustain-able Communities Initiative, Casius Pealer of the U.S. Green Building Council, Cameron Sinclair and Kate Stohr of Architecture for Humanity, Katie Swenson of the Enterprise Rose Fellowship, Barbara Wilson of the University of Texas at Austin, Jennifer Wolch of the University of California, Berkeley, Jocelyn Wyatt of IDEO, and Jess Zimbabwe of the Urban Land Institute.

Mentors Jim Cramer of the Design Futures Council, Tom Fisher at the University of Minnesota, Aaron Hurst of the Taproot Foundation, Reed Kroloff of the Cranbrook Academy of Art and Art Museum, and Raymond Lifchez at the University of California, Berkeley, have been some of the biggest proponents of Public Architecture and this book. Other supporters did everything from penning recommendation letters to providing counsel and a sounding board when I needed it most. They include Ava Abramowitz, Phil Bernstein, Ron Bogle, Adele Chatfield-Taylor, Dorothy Dunn, Fausto Giaccone, Clark Kellogg, Jere and Ron Martin, Trappeur Rahn, Scot Refsland, Wendy and Peter Rolland, Lisa Spinali, RK Stewart, Chuck Sullivan, Susan Szenasy, Paul Tractenberg, and Sally Young.

On a personal note, deep thanks go to my five siblings and their supportive spouses and children. My parents, Mary and John Cary, will always be both my personal and professional role models. Special thanks go to Michelle Cartier for always believing in me, and to Stephanie Malia Hom for showing me the world. Many peers offered vital encouragement as I wrote this book, including Melissa Burnett, Ellen Cathey, Laura Crescimano, Ray Dehn, Jenn Gee, Chris Goblet, Jamie Hartman, Zach Heineman, Tia Keobounpheng, Aaron Koch, Jon Lundstrom, Kirin Makker, Jody McGuire, Lisa Monzon, Godwin Moy, Amit Price Patel, Kelly Rittenhouse, Phoebe Schenker, Marika Shiori-Clark, and Susan Stinson.

Work on this book began in earnest in 2009, halfway around the world, when I held the Public Affairs Practitioner Residency at the Rockefeller Foundation's Bellagio Center in Italy. The time I spent there afforded the distance and reflection that I needed to understand pro bono design as a movement in the making. During that month and many that followed, I learned more about what it means to be a leader, a listener, and a storyteller from my Bellagio neighbor Courtney Martin, who provided unmatched care, counsel, and support throughout the process of publishing this book.

Together the stories presented and the countless individuals named and unnamed in these pages embody the social art of architecture. Public Architecture and I gratefully dedicate The Power of Pro Bono to these pioneering members of the pro bono movement.

About the Contributors

Majora Carter

founded and served as executive director of the nonprofit Sustainable South Bronx from 2001 to 2008, working to achieve environmental justice through economically sustainable projects that are informed by community needs. Her work now, as president of the Majora Carter Group, includes advising businesses, foundations, universities, and cities around the world on how to unlock their green-collar economic potential to benefit as many people as possible. Majora has earned numerous awards, including a MacArthur Fellowship, as well as recognition as one of *Essence* magazine's "25 Most Influential African-Americans" and inclusion on *Newsweek*'s list of "25 To Watch." She is a co-host on the Sundance Channel's series *The Green* and hosts a special public radio series called *The Promised Land*.

John Cary

served as executive director of Public Architecture from 2003 to 2010. He consults, speaks, and writes extensively on the intersection of design and service. In 2006, at age twenty-nine, he became the youngest person ever recognized as a Senior Fellow of the Design Futures Council, alongside nine building industry and environmental leaders including Nobel laureates Al Gore and Steven Chu. A Fellow of the American Academy in Rome, John was a 2008 recipient of the Rome Prize fellowship in design. He has also held the Public Affairs Practitioner Residency at the Rockefeller Foundation's Bellagio Center, and was among the inaugural class of fellows of the Aspen Institute's Ideas Festival. In 2009, he was recognized alongside John Peterson with the Designer of the Year Award from *Contract* magazine.

John Peterson

founded Public Architecture in 2002 and joined its staff full-time as president in 2008. He is also the principal of Peterson Architects, which, for many years, undertook extensive pro bono work for arts organizations, community development corporations, and social service agencies. John is a registered architect and a member of the American Institute of Architects (AIA), has served on several local nonprofit boards, and has held three mayoral task-force appointments in San Francisco. He is the recipient of multiple awards, including the Nice Modernist award from *Dwell* magazine in 2005, as well as local, state, and national citations from the AIA. John was a 2006 Loeb Fellow at the Harvard University Graduate School of Design.

Public Architecture

is a 501(c)(3) nonprofit organization established in 2002 that acts as a catalyst for public discourse through education, advocacy, and the design of public spaces and amenities. The 1% program of Public Architecture challenges architecture and design professionals to dedicate a minimum of 1 percent of their time to pro bono work, serving nonprofit arts organizations, community centers, health clinics, libraries, schools, and social service agencies in low-income communities across the country. The more than 750 architecture and design firms that are part of The 1% program have pledged to complete over $25 million in pro bono services annually. Public Architecture's design initiatives have been the subject of extensive press, including a National Geographic Channel documentary. Its work was featured in the Cooper-Hewitt National Design Museum's exhibition *Design for the Other 90%* and has received two international awards from the Holcim Foundation for Sustainable Construction. www.publicarchitecture.org

Credits